Repeating the Korean
Economic Miracle

# NEW WEALTH
# OF NATIONS

Repeating the Korean
Economic Miracle

# NEW WEALTH
## OF NATIONS

By **Ungsuh Kenneth Park**

DAEYANG MEDIA

# Introduction

Korea is a paradox. All odds were against its existence as a free democratic nation, but it still exists. General Douglas McArthur said it will take more than 100 years for Korea to recover from the rabbles of the Korean War. Winston Churchill said about defending democracy in Korea that it is like expecting a rose to grow out of a trash bin. But Korea has become the 8th largest economy[1] in the world unwaveringly keeping its democratic system strong, actually thriving because of this system, in the 71-year period since the war began.

Lester Thurow, the late dean of MIT Sloan School of Business reported in his book, *Head to Head: The Coming Economic Battle Among Japan, Europe, and America* (1993) that during the last one hundred years, from among the top twenty rich countries of the world only two Latin American countries dropped out and the vacancy was occupied by Japan and Kuwait. Japan was one of the richest

---

[1] During the corona pandemic Italy and Brazil slipped down below Korea, but they climbed back above Korea.

countries even before the statistics were compiled and Kuwait became rich through oil discoveries. In other words, rich is rich and poor is poor and the wall in between is not to be breached.

Just as white is not black, a poor person remains poor, and a weak country remains weak. Nobody lends capital to the hopeless poor countries and poor countries remain poor as we see them all over the world. This is like a natural law, or the law of gravity, which man may challenge but only temporarily. Going against this wisdom is a manifestation of stupidity. If any country challenges this impossible task and comes out with a victory, it will be recorded as a *paradox*, for this country turned impossibility into a possibility. We call this a miracle.

More than a dozen publicly funded Korean economic research institutes and the same number of private economic institutions continues producing endless reports about the Korean economy and its changes, mostly in Korean language. The OECD and UN organizations put out reports containing Korean economic statistics in minute detail. The media casually complements Korea using words like 'miracle' and 'amazing' after superficial observations. Academics who should trace the causes of the 'miracle' are very uncomfortable with that word, and their disciplines are so compartmentalized that their minds cannot reach beyond separately viewing the rapid changes in economic growth, the history of democracy, and the process of ensuring the deterrence of war as unrelated individual phenomena. That sort of approach will never explain the miracle. In spite of the glut of reports on the Korean economy, there exists a big empty vacancy looking for a readable and integral report of this subject written in plain English. This book is written to fill this gap.

When Korea was liberated from Japanese imperial rule in 1945, I was in my first year of elementary school, and I barely understood the concept of freedom. However, as I went into university it came as a shock to me to find out that Korea was poorer than the poorest countries in Africa and South Asia. In my lifetime, Korea was invaded by the Japanese, Chinese, and North Koreans. In my father's lifetime Korea was invaded by the Chinese, Russians, French, English, Japanese, and even by Americans. It was raided and pillaged by foreigners and Japan even tried to extinguish our language and heritage to prove that Korea is not ready for independence. I still remember my Japanese name, surname included, that I was required to use in order to enter primary school. Korea was described by a poet as 'my mother, a ragged but beautiful woman, lying at the western corner of the Pacific Ocean after repeated rapes and violence'. How can one resist loving and caring for this poor mother?

In Korea, we achieved a free democracy with a strong enough military deterrence blessed with a prosperous economy. We did this on incredibly harsh terrain, despite the fact that we are surrounded by hostile powers that are ranked 2nd, 3rd , and 5th in the world in military power. For Korea remaining poor and weak, while being independent was an unsustainable luxury, because our hostile neighbors would have turned us into colonial slaves with a commu-nist touch. The existential threat was and probably is the strongest motivation and source of energy for becoming a rich and powerful nation. In this sense, Korea was lucky to be under constant threat from China, North Korea, and the Soviet Union, even by Japan. This is the worst kind of paradox for Korea. In a paradoxical way, Korea's rapid development owes a lot to the unending threats from its neighbors.

Living next to China is a painful experience. China's large land mass, population, and military power are the source of constant security instability. China has three times the population of the entire population of Europe with a land mass similar to Europe. As the basis of peace, Europe enjoys a stable structure of power balance among 28 countries. No single state can prevail over all of them. Two great wars and the Cold War proved that. Asia can never enjoy lasting peace until either China is disintegrated into a dozen countries, or the one-and-a-half billion Chinese people understand that their Sino-Centrism is the greatest obstruction to the continuous prosperity of China.

China's national goal manifested directly by the government spokesman is that it becomes the center of the world, and ensures that *lesser countries* become subservient. The Foreign Affairs spokesman demanded that "Small states should respect the will of big states" with no hesitation, while at the same time claiming that "China never seeks hegemony." Winston Churchill would have loved to call that giant greed wrapped in colossal hypocrisy. The magnificent technological progress of the 21st century in digital connectivity has only intensified the temptation of the Big Brother Communist Party leaders.

Korea has transformed itself in three dimensions simultaneously by building (1) strong defensive power for military deterrence to maintain peace, (2) a sound democratic system that ensures individual freedom, basic human rights, and social transparency through freedom of expression, and (3) a prosperous economy achieved by private property ownership and a market economy. A *Trinity Theory of National Development* follows, namely that a national development comes in a set of three simultaneous accomplishments; peace, freedom, and prosperous market economy. The absence of any one of the three practically prevents lasting national development, and three of them together constitute the necessary conditions for successful development.

The main course of this recipe for national development is the Korean experience rather than theorizing it. This book is an anatomy of what is loosely called the Korean

Miracle. It is the wish of this author that all the developing countries and their leaders get some help or hint from this book in designing and carrying out their task of nation-building.

# Contents

Contents

# Unique Trajectory

# Is Korea Going Anywhere?

# I. The Korea Paradox

Ⅰ. The Korea Paradox

# I. The Korea Paradox

## Paradox of Impossible Tasks

Korean economic development is a story of building up a system of independent self-defense against the never-ending communist threat from countries with nuclear weapons. It is a story of creating an economic system large and strong enough to equip the military with the most powerful destructive firepower and most accurate interception capability to stop incoming missiles. It is a story of creating a pool of highly capable human resources to compete in the most advanced high-tech industries, where new technologies are not shared but must be acquired by one's own research. It is a story of creating a set of world-class corporations starting from primitive merchants who had no manufacturing experience. It is a story of creating millions of happy middle-class people who participate not only in the process of creating wealth but possess the wealth they created. All these accomplishments started at a thoroughly devastated land filled with starving people with a very low level of education and civic morality. Even to the eyes of this witness, expecting to succeed in these paradoxical tasks was unreasonable, to say the least. Only a miracle could bring success.

The most extraordinary part of the Korean miracle is that we had to push the economy through militaristic social regimentation at the beginning. However, today we are regarded as the one and only success story of a free market economy that escaped from the world's worst poverty and became one of the richest countries all under a democratic political system with a transparent and free press. Achieving economic prosperity was the easy part when compared to the creation of an effective and sufficiently strong military deterrence that prevents a war on this Peninsula. We had to build the world's top retaliatory capability for any surprise attacks, sufficient to dissuade our enemies from acting rashly.[2] If we failed, we would have to return to a system of national slavery. Political scientists call it Fin-

---

[2] The fundamental disparity of the situation comes from the fact that we do not want to invade our neighbors or make first-strike attacks while our neighbors do.

landization. But Finlandization living next to China is no better than Tibetization. Our semiconductor technology became the national target for China to sustain its hegemonic contest against the USA. The world's largest semiconductor fab owner, TSMC of Taiwan, makes Taiwan the most attractive target for invasion by China.

Korea had nothing at the beginning except its people and bare mountains. It is well known that South Korea was endowed with close to zero natural resources and virtually no industrial facilities at the end of the 36 years of brutal Japanese colonial rule. In retrospect, we were wrong. Korea was endowed with 30 million illiterate but hard-working people who were groundlessly proud and self-confident. They turned out our best resource. The next chapter on Korean obsession with education, and equally obsessive technology competition will explain how Korea turned the ignorant farmers into industrial assets and made the value of the people expensive.

Half of the government budget after the Korean War was provided by the sales revenue of US aid in the form of grains and raw sugar under Public Law 480. The other half came from a counter-fund raised by the internal tax. The national budget had to be screened, item by item, by the US AID officers stationed in Korea before being submitted to the National Assembly. One may wonder why the US Embassy building is located amongst the Korean government buildings right in front of Kyung Bok Place. US AID officers had two identical buildings designed and built, one to be used by the Korean Reconstruction Ministry that made the budget, and the other by US AID to oversee the budget.[3] Seven years after the cease-fire agreement, the Korean government was still not able to finance its government budget through internal tax revenue. Korea exported 20 million dollar worth of fishery products and tungsten ores. The Student Revolution of 1960 brought down the government and entailed nationwide chaos. We needed a strong leadership.

On April 1, 1961, I started my first job as a young economist at the Bank of Korea, the central bank, just recruited from the graduate class of the economics department of Seoul National University. Barely one month later, on May

---

[3] The US Embassy is now using the AID Building and the other building is now occupied by the Korean Culture and Sports Ministry.

16, a group of senior officers of the Korean army successfully staged a military *coup d'etat* and took over the government. They ran the country for 18 years. The first public pledge of their Revolutionary Manifesto was, "Anti-Communism shall be the prime national creed", followed by the second pledge, "Economic development shall be our prime target and shall be achieved through modernization of our society." At our research department of the Bank, we were ordered to key in all sorts of economic and social data in the 'Monroe Machine', as we used to call the heavy and noisy desk calculator that was as big as the present-day cathode ray tube computer monitors, to determine the length of time required to double our GDP. Three months later the First Five-Year Plan of Economic and Social Development was proclaimed by the military government as the guideline for the future economic management of the country.

That was the signal of a great change in Korean society and economy. Hardly anyone outside Korea was interested in these changes that turned out to be the genesis of a great transformation of an exceptionally poor and devastated country into one of the richest countries in the world. History has many examples in which a poor savage army conquered rich countries and became rich rulers, but Korea is the first example of a country that created wealth through fair competition and technological development in the open global economy without a military invasion and colonial exploitation. We performed this miracle while at the same time fighting against an authoritarian government. Korea set up a reasonably functioning democratic system and achieved mass prosperity for millions of children of former serfs, and exploited tenants. This book is an eyewitness account of this great transformation.

In 2021, 60 years later, I am typing this book on my desktop PC, with absolutely no physical discomforts typical to octogenarians, still wondering how this metamorphosis of Korea was possible. People call it a miracle. I think it a revolution that uprooted and demolished the old regime and concepts of the interrelationship between people, traditional government practices, the entrenched poverty, national security, and self-respect.

Amazingly throughout the changes either during the rapid economic growth under a strong government or slow growth under a weak government, Koreans never lost the sense of unity that bound the people together in one big communitarian society with a common objective. The dynamic energy that created present Korea seems to continue even now. Its strength in bonding the people and corporations together is still creating a new unknown economy and society.


## A New Narrative

So much has been written and published on the miracle of Korean economic development already and there does not seem to be much left that will interest the readers. Large volumes of literature however did not succeed in explaining this unique and unprecedented miracle in human history; the miracle of transforming the poorest and virtually demolished country into one of the richest nations in the world under a free democratic political system. In fact calling it a miracle is irresponsible, for it is the same as saying that it should not have happened but if it did, it is beyond any rational explanation within economic theories. Just as water should have remained water instead of turning into wine two thousand years ago in Israel, Korea should have remained poor and weak. Therefore calling it a miracle is equivalent to renouncing a rational explanation. I will explain why this miracle was inevitable and show readers that the history and trajectory of this miracle is loaded with explanations about why each step of the changes was perfectly rational and inevitable.

I will attempt to conduct a mental anatomy of the social disintegration of Korea, a process of parts, or sectors, escaping from one big suffocating and stagnating equilibrium. We will see the roads, and the dynamic paths of each part of the society that survived overwhelming destructions, military as well as economic, and how they arrived at the final destiny, separately and interactively. Call it modernity or mass prosperity if you like. One by one they eventually formed a new organic equilibrium. When the parts finally assembled together, we were astonished by the amazing miraculous results.

In this analysis, I will largely disregard the chronology of Korean development history, and examine the causes and consequences of the significant changes of the important parts of society. Obviously, major changes took place in lumps creating some form of epoch and I will explain them in order. Without exception, I discovered that each and every part that underwent significant changes was in a self-contradictory paradox, and keeping it unchanged would have been harder than letting it change. This is what I call the social energy crammed underneath, waiting for the time to explode. The more powerful the paradoxes that are pent up, the easier it is to bring change to the economy and society. But it comes with the enormous risk of wrecking the society and system. Only a select few managed to arrive at a new path of growth and development.

In this analysis I will largely disregard the chronology of the Korean development history, and examine the causes and consequences of the significant changes of the important parts of society. Obviously major changes took place in lumps creating some form of epoch and I will explain them in order. Without exception, I discovered that each and every part that underwent significant changes was in a self-contradictory paradox, and keeping it unchanged would have been harder than letting it change. This is what I call the social energy crammed underneath waiting for the time to explode. The more powerful the paradoxes that are pent up, the easier it is to bring change to the economy and society. But it comes with the enormous risk of wrecking the society and system. Only a selected few managed to come on a new path of growth and development.

I must warn the readers that I will not regurgitate the statistical empiricism, for we all know what happened. Statistics are products of compromises made by collectors and collators, and they frequently reflect government aspirations. Any pretention of precision when using official statistics gets close to hypocrisy. I will help you to develop an understanding of how differently Koreans thought and behaved at each crisis and major event.

## Paradox, Mother of All Miracles

We do not need Friedrich Hegel and his dialectics to understand that a prominent paradox in any society is a sign that this society is packed with a high level of energy to facilitate change. A boulder sitting on flat ground has no kinetic energy but a boulder at the tip of the cliff has enormous potential kinetic energy. A little push from behind can give the boulder devastating energy that can crush an entire town below the cliff. A poor country full of angry citizens is like a scene where many boulders are waiting to be pushed down to crush the entire town below.

Some societies have been poor and deprived for thousands of years and people generally take it for granted that it is their destiny to be born and live poor. But some societies discover that they are relatively poor compared to the colonial rulers or prosperous neighbors who used to be just as poor as themselves. In many traditional societies, a profound sense of despair and hopelessness prevails as people realize that they have severely limited resources and impotent leaders. People frequently take poverty as karma. But in some societies, dissatisfaction and anger boil up to create the storm that pushes the boulders down the cliff. This is the antithesis, and antithesis is the manifestation of an existing paradox.

This paradox can intensify until the synthetic outcome causes a total annihilation of the stagnant old society and pushes the country back to the medieval ages. Usually, this is the normal case and many poor countries that relied on the communist revolution to cut the old shackles went through this unfortunate regression. When the social kinetic energy of poverty and anger erupts, it can become violent and brutal characterized by many riots. Not all states can return to normalcy as quickly as the USA after violent riots. Many rioters create an insurgent power and divide the nation for, say, rights of natural resource exploitation for minerals and mines of diamonds, which occurred in Sierra Leon. Hegel will love this synthesis of divided nations killing each other, for it proves that when the old paradox is crushed, it creates a new paradox, and his dialectics continue.

Korea was a colonial society intensely exploited by the Japanese imperialistic government until the end of WWII and it was one of the poorest countries in the world when it was liberated. Furthermore, it went through a war that destroyed almost any structures except old palaces, thank God. To old soldiers who fought during the Korean War, and to all Koreans who experienced the war including this author, achieving a prosperous country within three generrations in this devastated land would have sounded like a daydream. But Korea not only achieved world-class prosperity but also is regularly invited to the G7 Summit Meetings, the exclusive organization of the richest and strongest free nations of the world. As the Ukraine war exhausted the American supply capacity of interception missiles, Korea is slowly turning into the only viable alternative arsenal of high-tech weapons outside the USA to the East European countries who became visibly nervous about the possible Russian invasion. If anybody predicted three generations ago that something like this would occur, his mental sanity would have been suspected. But this miracle became a reality. It doesn't look rational. but it happened. It is a paradox and miracle?[4]

We will see in Korea two broad streams of changes on a national scale. The first is the amazing change *in the People*. When the country became independent, 80% of the population was serfs and poor tenant farmers without any asset ownership. For thousand years, they were the victims of exploitation by the aristocrats of Korea. The Korean development process forcefully turned them into an asset-owning middle class and put them through mandatory

---

[4] One dictionary defines paradox as a situation or statement that seems impossible or is difficult to understand because it contains two opposite facts or characteristics. Another says it is a statement that runs contrary to one's expectation. I am not sure if I agree with this definition. Another says it is a statement that, despite apparently valid reasoning from true premises, leads to a seemingly self-contradictory or a logically unacceptable conclusion. This one has many holes.

education. Without electricity at home, their children had to walk to school miles away, and as the economy is industrialized, these children became corporate managers, professors, lawyers, labor union members, and managerial staff in project sites all over the world. Their grandchildren became owners of urban properties worth millions of dollars as the economy entered into mature industrial and post-industrial society all in a matter of three generations. It is a story of how the economic value of the ordinary Korean people rose by a factor of 1000 times. It is a story of how Korean workers who were forced to work longer hours than any other people in the world continuously chose a democratic political system that continues to pursue economic growth more than equity.

The second amazing stream of change is *Commerce*. The Japanese colonial government prohibited Koreans from incorporating any modern business and when Korea was liberated all Korean businessmen operated as single merchants or small groups of partners for importing corn and bean from Manchuria (Samsung), or for car repairing (Hyundai). When they were asked to form modern corporations to take up the projects of the First Five-Year Plan (textiles, consumer chemicals, construction of highways, etc.), they had to be forced to cooperate with the new military government. In about sixty years, they became challengers to the best and most powerful corporations of the world in semiconductors, electric cars and lithium batteries, shipbuilding of LNG carriers, and scram-jet torpedoes that dash underwater at 500 km per hour. This is a story of how these reluctant merchants became global leaders of modern technology in rolling TV screens, foldable mobile phones, LED displays with over-hundred million pixels, and even automatic mobile long range howitzers, taking 80% of the world market.

This is an epic story of the Republic of Korea. The story is not a narrative of the developmental path of Korea. Instead, this book attempts to determine the major essential paradoxes that made the Korean miracle inevitable. It is a story of boulders that used to stand on the hill threatening the city and how the people below turned the boulders into monuments that they cannot forget. It is a story of how they built their own powerful social energy that prevented the boulders from destroying their city by raising the ground level of the city higher than the boulders and neutralizing the dangerous potential kinetic energy.

## Dignified Poverty and the Ultimate Paradox

Four children from elementary school to high school and their parents all sleeping in a small room with one meal a day was not the life of the poorest of Korean society in 1946 to 55. It was the life of middle-class families. Unlike most Korean fathers who did not have proper jobs that paid steady salaries, my father was a bank clerk with a BA degree from a university in Japan. The poverty in Korea was epidemic, and winter morning newspapers routinely reported the number of people who were frozen to death or died because of hunger, or both with no names. Death was mere statistic.

Poverty is not new to Koreans. For thousands of years to the landless tenant farmers or serfs, poverty was a destiny. Monarchs who needed the loyalty of landed aristocrats didn't do much to deter the cruel exploitations of commoners by landowners. That's normal. But in the case of Korea, even landed class became poor, for many land owners, who failed to produce legally acceptable documented evidence of land ownership conforming Japanese laws, since 1910, the Japanese colonial government confiscated them.

Poverty was respected in old Korea. This is one major paradox. I am not aware of any culture where poverty is glorified. But for centuries, Koreans were educated to be proud of poverty until the Japanese rule and Korean War woke them up to the fact that poverty does not protect them from invasion, but prosperity, or at least money, or economic power does. Traditionally poverty was regarded as the inevitable consequence of honorable and honest public life, and Confucius scholars who filled most of the bureaucratic positions were educated to live in an honorable poverty.

But after 500 years, this culture regressed into institutionalized hypocrisy. This hypocritical culture of honorable poverty left a pernicious bias among the educated class to shun and hold in contempt any profession seeking profit. Wealth earned by serving the Japanese colonial rulers by comprador capitalists only intensified the contempt of wealth and pride in poverty. King Sejong who invented one of the most scientific writing systems in the world, greatly admired a serf whose name was Young Shil Jang, a brilliant scientist and engineer. The king appointed him as his closest assistant. But the bureaucrats pressured and cornered the king to banish him and give permission to the rigid bureaucrats to burn all of his research works. The egotistic aristocrats claimed that the pragmatic research results not only distracted the king who needed to concentrate on the noble scholarly humanities and classic literature but also made the lives of serfs and farmers *too comfortable* and thereby making them unruly over time. That was the sin.

Economic growth requires people who want to escape poverty, but if the people are brainwashed into considering poverty as honorable, then there is no hope. It would certainly be a paradox if growth took place in such a country. In Korean traditional ethics, gentlemen or intellectuals should look at a bar of gold as a rock and any aristocrat who fails to withstand the temptation of material well-being should not take public office.[5] How could we teach

---

[5] Interestingly the Japanese Samurai class also entertained contempt against profit-seeking professions. But the land-owning aristocrats and merchants had to create symbiotic relationships to support the endless war against neighboring feudal Daimyos. This suddenly stopped when the samurais lost their jobs after their boss Daimyos lost their manors to the army of Emperor Meiji at the time of modernization. Some of these roaming residual Samurais became the founding fathers of Mitsubishi and Mitsui Jaibatzu

them what they need is economic growth, and to escape from poverty? If we succeeded in economic growth then that is against common sense and it is, indeed, a good paradox. The biggest paradox is that this millennium-old traditional value system was instantly destroyed by a war that nearly erased this country from the map.

What turned the old Koreans from their ancient hypocritical poverty worship into cargo-worshipping materialists? The answer is the Korean War. Throughout Korean history never had the whole Peninsula been so completely devastated from the northern end to the southern end by the world's most powerful air force in pursuit of 400,000 Chinese ground troops equipped with heavy artillery captured from the Japanese army at the end of WWII in Manchuria. South Korean soldiers had only M1 rifles. After the nationwide devastation caused by the Korean War, all 30 million Koreans became equally poor except perhaps a few, less than 50 families, I presume, and the nation realized that every single citizen stood at the same starting line of a race to prosperity. The last drop of remaining mental class con-

---

Groups, Japan's first commercial ship owners, or even formed the powerful Yakuza (organized crime) groups, but they have mostly disappeared.

sciousness and ancestral privilege disappeared completely and former serfs, aristocrats, and scholars did not hesitate to use violence to grab any last piece of bread. Jungle rules prevailed during the war, and after the war, for 90% of Koreans, there was no employment except for some public service jobs and school teachers. School teachers? Yes school teachers. We will have to talk about this obsession with education by Koreans, for this is one of the most important paradoxes and sources of energy in the Korean development story.

## The New Religion of Materialism

More importantly, Koreans suddenly realized that they were not capable of manufacturing a single rifle when the Northern army invaded with tanks and artillery provided by the USSR, the former bigger version of Russia. A *Rich Nation and Strong Military* became a new national goal and the fundamental basis of a new morality. Poverty suddenly became a sin and complacency became a cause of shame. The spirit of the Mayflower finally arrived on the Korean shore with its Protestant ethics. In fact, Christianity which had a significant following only in the Northwestern part of Korea, where this author is from, became the predominant religion for 13 million adults, and it became the basis of conservative politics here. Apparently, it takes nationwide devastation to crash an entrenched paradox on a national scale.

After the war, people suddenly became aware of the shameful ranking of Korean poverty that the United Nations statistics reported. Before the war Koreans were largely ignorant about the UN, let alone its statistics. Now they came to know that poverty is an indignity or even a sin. It causes children to suffer, and there is nothing to be proud of. The dividing line of morality had shifted, and the shameless pursuit of material well-being became almost moral in this new culture that the UN Armed Forces brought to this Peninsula with their colorful magazines and films.

One may say a thousand words explaining that only a strong military deterrence can keep peace and that only a rich industrial country can afford strong armed forces. But it cannot match one big destructive war in convincing people that we need to be rich and powerful to keep the peace.

The cursed location of Korea provided a great service in facilitating Korea's modernization through the equally cursed Korean War. This is a paradox among paradoxes. People realized what we need was not honor but wealth and modern industry.

Old values became mere burdens in life, and old histories of weakness and poverty became objects of ridicule. People took pride in doing things differently and were thrilled to violate old rules, especially laws and ethics. So many nights around US military bases, empty drum cans rolled down the hill by themselves while the guards who were bribed beforehand turned their heads in other directions. Korea couldn't produce a rifle let alone an automobile. But the drum cans were resurrected into metal skins of buses with power trains taken from old *written-off* GMC military trucks, which in fact were brand new trucks, just arrived on shore from the USA. Thousands of buses filled the city streets for urban public transportation in major cities, and they were not imported for sure.

This process of constructing a new materially bountiful society from the rubbles of the war and ashes of a destroyed value and culture system demanded dedication by its people, and strong trust that the new society of their dreams would be realized. Like a pagan religious ceremony that demanded human blood, this new religion of materialism jealously demanded full attention and dedication. Koreans were ready to give up anything for the promise of prosperity, which their former rulers and religion failed to provide. The new rule of market competition under a democratic government was nothing less than a great new Messianic promise of biblical importance to them. No less than the United Nations, the strongest military of the United States, and the sixteen countries that sent troops, all to defend our democracy from communism confirmed that this new religion is just the right one for Koreans. We didn't have to be ashamed of pursuing materialism openly and the institution of democracy and the market economy seemed so appropriate.

Under the murderous desert heat of Middle Eastern construction sites, in the deadly shrubs of the equatorial jungles of Vietnam, in the suffocating coal mines 200 meters below ground in Germany, and in numerous other venues and circumstances, where economic values were created, Korean youth, who are now 70 to 90 years of age, gladly gave their labor together with their lives. At three a.m. in the morning, they went back to their Middle-Eastern construction sites because the desert temperature was just right to work and woke them up. The quicker the project was finished the earlier they could go home.

In the sweatshops of garment factories in Seoul, and on the icy decks of tuna ships on the coast of Southern Chile, they gladly worshipped the Goddess of Abundance. Time Magazine invented a new term 'Reverse Brain Drain' reporting the totally irrational behavior of intelligent Koreans who elected to return home giving up safe positions in the US and West where they were paid 6 figure salaries. In spite of the 20-some years of authoritarian military rule, or perhaps because of it, people had zero suspicion about economic success. Mr. Kim Woo Jung, the founder chairman of Daewoo Group who was one year older than this author, famously remarked "The world is huge and filled with work to be done." The Korean cult of materialism and prosperity was so contagious that even our communist neighbor, China decided to emulate it.

On an electronic scoreboard hung on top of a building near the Nam Dae Mun Gate, the accumulated annual total of export value in dollars was displayed day and night for all worshippers to follow. Reports of landing big orders in construction, civil engineering, huge cross harbor bridges, the world's largest container carriers, oil tankers, huge refineries, and land reclaiming projects that altered maps and geography became a source of fun and thrill for Koreans, although many knew this would delay the return of their husbands, brothers, and sons. There was very little doubt that the ultimate beneficiary of the national economic growth would be the people themselves. We will come back to this claim.

## Constant Threat, the Blessing in Disguise

Korean farmers raise mudfish in the rice paddies when they are full of water in summer. Some farmers put catfish in the pad with the mudfish. Catfish may hunt and take several mudfish but the mudfish the farmers are able to harvest are bigger, fatter, and more delicious with better meat quality. Only the highest-quality mudfish survive the constant hunting and attacks by dangerous catfish. For nearly a century, North Korea devotes all of its national resources to purchasing and deploying the most advanced missiles and developing weapons of mass destruction such as nuclear bombs and chemical weapons for the sole purpose of annexing South Korea, which they call unification.

Korea's biggest and nearest neighbor, China, actually invaded Korea in 1950 and fought against the Korean army and UN Armed Forces for more than 3 years. The supreme leader of the Chinese Communist Party (CCP), Mr. Xi, Jin Ping announced in the last week of March 2021, that if the South Korean army invades North Korea, China will immediately dispatch its armed forces to the DMZ to defend his dear friend Kim, Jeong Eun.

Right-wing political leaders of Japan never hesitate to confess that the best tonic for rejuvenating the Japanese economy is to start another war on the Korean Peninsula. Many intelligent Japanese believe that the right-wing extremists of Japan use "Hate Korea" policy and slogans to keep their rate of public popularity high. Whenever Korean industries such as semiconductors or lithium batteries surpass Japan's in technological advancement or international competitiveness, the Hate-Korea campaign seems to intensify.[6]

Korea is surrounded by powerful, actual, and potential enemies GDPs of whom rank second, third and 10th in the world. Nowhere in the world, there is a country surrounded by global giants with military firepower ranking number two, three, and five, all ready to send their army to this peninsula. The calamitous geopolitical position of Israel is like a peaceful spring-day dream compared to the danger that Korea faces. Visitors to Korea should wonder about the composure that Korean people show under these tense circumstances. Even at this moment, Korean soldiers on the southern side of the DMZ[7] stand guard 24/7 against the possible Northern invasion which can take place any time

---

[6] In August, 2019 the Japanese government suddenly banned free exports of critical materials needed in manufacturing semiconductor memory chips. Export of the memory chips is one of Korea's life-supporting economic activities. The chips are produced in circuitry of 5 nanometer width and in more than a hundred stories of circuits stacked up on a fingernail-sized space with a height of less than two millimeters. The official explanation for the ban was that Korea may export the same material to enemy countries for military purposes. Such re-export has never happened either before or after the ban. Japan has still not lifted the case-by-case permission system used by their bureaucracy.

[7] The Demilitarized Zone was set up by an agreement between the UN armed forces and North Korea/China representatives in July 1953. The DMZ divided the Korean Peninsula into two halves, and it has been divided since then.

without warning. Strangely even visitors seem to forget that they are in a country where war is halted temporarily. Imagine living in a cease-fire situation for 68 years and three generations. This is not normal.

Korea arguably is the most infertile terrain in the world for planting the seed for economic growth. There was virtually no indigenous capital to play the role of a pump primer, domestic technology was practically nonexistent, there was hardly any market for manufactured goods due to the exceptionally low national income, and there were no entrepreneurs to put strategic resources together for business objectives. We only had a *Plan and People*. Expecting successful economic development and sustained growth was a paradox,

But the people who were like the mudfish constantly chased by the catfish found there was no alternative but to trust the government's plans and dedicate their labor, talents, and resources to the commonly accepted economic goals of the community. In other words, the series of the Five-Year Economic and Social Plans and government allocation of investment capital was a strong assurance to the business community that the industrial captains would receive all the necessary assistance from the government if they followed the planned trajectories. Abnormally high investment risk that drives foreign investors away justified an abnormally strong government and hard-handed economic policy, plus ample assistance. Actually, people preferred it. The military government, which managed the first two economic plans successfully, self-justified their strong ruling by the *legitimacy by the delivery* of economic success.

# The Groundworks

# II. Obsession with Education

## Mandatory Education, the First Step to Prosperity

There are three main pillars that constitute the basis upon which modern Korean society was constructed through sustained economic development. They are mandatory education, land reform, and the Korean War. In this chapter we will look into the extraordinary demand for education by Korean parents and society. Many writers claim that the thousand-year long tradition of examinations to obtain public offices, which was the only way to rise to aristocracy, brewed the excess demand for education. But Korea is not the only country where elites were selected through examinations, but not all of them succeeded in economic development.

Over 80% of the population was farmer in Korea at the

beginning ie.1945. Land reform turned them overnight into independent, risk-taking, income-maximizing agro-ventures. The Korean War exposed them to what was happening outside Korea, especially in the USA and Europe. Old ways and culture were revered in farming, irrigation, construction, calendar-making, and a prudent life but our farmers discovered that their ways brought only poverty compared to the modern farming technology of the West. Now what they needed was a bridge to connect them to a different system, the knowhow and technology that the farmers of rich countries use. Obviously education was the missing link.

The Korean constitution states that all citizens have rights to receive equal free education depending on individual ability. Furthermore, in the Basic Law of Education 1949, it is specified that all citizens are entitled to mandatory education for six years elementary school and three years of middle school. The commencement of the mandatory education for middle school was to be determined by the president of the Republic in consideration of the budgetary situation. This decision was made in 1948, the same year when the constitution was written, for a country with a per capita GDP below one hundred US dollar per year.

A system of mandatory education has three elements; parental responsibility to send the children to school, regional governments' responsibility to build and run schools of adequate size in convenient locations for children, as well as to recruit teachers, and the role of the central government to provide a budget sufficient enough for the system to function properly. For this purpose a law requiring Educational Tax, and a law setting up Educational Grants for Regional Administrations were legislated at the same time. But due to the tight budget situation during the Korean war, that started right after the legislation, mandatory education applied only to six years of primary school children as soon as the armistice took place. This author is one of the first batches of beneficiaries of this system and the budgetary situation was so tight that our school won the honor of being the world's largest primary school.[8]

But from 1971 the number of primary students started

---

[8] The primary school that this author attended at the eastern suburb of Seoul had 20 classes for each grade and typical size of each class was just below one hundred children. Total number of students was over 10,000 and the classes were divided into those using class rooms, corridors, and the school ground with portable chalk boards on time sharing basis. We didn't know that this was abnormal. We were happy children.

to decline due to increased female employment opportunities in the urban industrial sector, and this pushed the average age of marriage upward, and lowered the birth rates. That gave a budgetary breath room and middle school level mandatory education started this year. The next step was mandatory high school education. Tuitions are now free for the three-year high school period, but not mandatory.

Education is an investment, for the wages paid to high-quality human resources that will be needed ten to twenty years later will also be very high. Furthermore, education takes the highest share of the central government budget, even higher than the defense and welfare budgets in middle income countries. Poor countries do not acquire expensive weapons, and soldiers are paid miserably low. Social welfare does not exist in practical terms until the economy reaches the middle-income level. All governments agree with this investment, and allocate the highest share of their budget to education. Governments that fail to allocate enough budget to education fail in development. This is the first rule of nation building. But public education is never sufficient compared to the needs of parents and industries.

Education helps to raise the quality of life of the people as income rises. As we will discuss more in the next chapter, lifting the economic value of people is the object of any national and economic development. Education is the means of development as well as the object of economic growth. My personal dream is to register at a university to learn music composition, but I haven't found the time for it yet. In this case education is a consumption activity, not directly connected to raising my income. Hence it is not a means of development. But when the economy is at an initial stage of development, education is an investment in most case.

Economic resources are acquired by paying the market price. This payment changes the ownership of the resource. The new owner may crush it or put them into furnace and squeeze out the final product or simply waste it. The new owner can do whatever he wants with it. But the knowledge that we obtain by investing in education is neither disposed of, nor consumed. It remains as part of the individual for a lifetime. And we value in markets a person with education higher than the uneducated. Education makes a person *better*. But strangely we call ourselves human *resources*, which sounds slightly denigrating. At any rate, Korea has no natural resources of any significant value except for the 30 million human resources.

Mandatory education increases the user value of human resources for it raises each worker's ability to learn new technology and increases dexterity. But in Korea education has become a national game involving competition for an undefined trophy that must be won for a very strange reason that the parents couldn't afford the education when they were young. In Korean it is called 'Mot Bae Woon Sorum' that roughly translates as the social stigma of the uneducated class. Poverty was a tolerable inconvenience but being uneducated was an unbearable stigma never to be passed on to the next generation. Being educated is the trophy itself.

## Unusual Hunger for Education

The literacy rate of countries is positively correlated with the level of national income. This is unchallengeable common sense for any society. No matter what statistics are used, the correlation is inescapable. Parents invest in education for their children after the basic necessities of family life are secured. If one reverses this order and educates children first while starving, we think this individual is abnormal or even crazy. This is another paradox that characterizes Korea. Koreans reverse this order habitually. Korea is an outlier on the scatter diagram of the literacy rate (y-axis) and level of national income (x-axis) for it stood out at the north western corner alone with an abnormally high literacy rate combined with a very low income level

For most parents in the world, primary school education is regarded as a consumption good and the expenses are usually paid for by the government. Secondary and upper level education is almost always regarded as an investment, and the parents think that the expense paid for upper level education is a tax-free inheritance that children are able to recover through their better future incomes. Of course parents' expectations are not always fulfilled.

There are several countries in the world with unusually high education levels. A large number of highly educated people is not easy to handle, if you are poor. Frequently in such countries the educated people turn into cynical intellectual groups that are highly vocal about their social discontent. Nearly half of the American intellectuals seem to support reducing the police department budget and seem to believe that tolerating violent riots on the street and rampages of private properties is better than tolerating police brutality. In the cost-minimizing market economy, over-educating children is not a good income allocation strategy. In Korea over-education demonstrated at least one very important positive social role, namely, it accelerated social changes by igniting the detonator of the pent-up social energy of dissatisfaction.

Mandatory national education is an expensive system for any poor stagnant economy, and no elected government would initiate this luxury as the first policy after inauguration. But in 1949 the Korean government passed the law to implement mandatory primary education, which was required by its constitution that had come into existence in the same year. For more than a thousand years in Korea education was the only ladder that provided upward social mobility. Bureaucracy, which was comprised of the aristocracy, maintained its system of recruiting fresh talent through two examinations, a humanity-classic exam and a military exam. But the enthusiasm for children's education among Korean parents was and is far beyond the normal global standard. Koreans are not offended if they are stigmatized as being crazy, when it comes to education.

## Origin of Higher Education in Korea

In 1952 the Korean War reached a swamp of a stalemate with no significant gains of land for either side, producing many uncountable and meaningless deaths. The entire nation was astonished when the president of South Korea, Dr. Syngman Rhee issued a shocking executive order that no university graduates or registered students should be drafted into the army. Although Seoul was recaptured from the Chinese and North Koreans by the United Nations Armed Forces, it was too dangerous for the government to return to Seoul, and it stayed in the city of Busan, just in case the capital city might be recaptured by the enemy.

His reasoning for such an unfair and unjust decision

was that the war would end one way or another, and if all the young men with or without education are killed as bullet fodders on the front lines, who would run the country? The political ramifications were extremely dangerous, for poor parents without money to pay the university tuitions had to give up their children to defend the country. Even for a junior high school kid, that was how old I was, this inequity was simply not acceptable. But there was neither a riot against this outrageous policy next morning, nor any mornings afterwards.

In retrospect, with this shocking and astonishing decision he outwitted the rest of us once again. He actually wanted fewer Korean kids to die on the front lines, and he wanted more young men from friendly countries, mostly the USA, to fill the shortages of conscription. He seemed to have no moral guilt on this point because it was the American government that was hesitant to win the war outright and free North Korea with its powerful superior weapons. Instead they negotiated for an armistice that dragged on and on for nearly two years, that produced greater sacrifice of lives. University registration soared, for any middle-class family with a young man of the right age gave up their normal meals and farmland to save the lives of their brothers and uncles.

Dr. Rhee, who American officers and diplomats called "the Old Fox", introduced another shocking rule. Universities that set up their temporary campuses of tents on top of windy Busan hills found the humanities and social science departments generated a healthy financial surplus from tuition income, but the engineering and science departments did not. All the universities tried to recruit only humanities and social science students and professors. The Ministry of Education declared an upper limit of 80% for entry into humanities and social sciences and demanded 20% of new students enroll in science and engineering. Thus Korean science and engineering education began by governmental coercion together with profit motivations of university 'owners' in the tertiary educational market. That 20/80 rule subsequently changed to 30/70, and over time eventually disappeared. Over half a century later, some of these universities that started on tent campuses grew to become globally known educational institutions and some of the regency chairmen or their children became rich and powerful Jaebol leaders of Korean community. Dr. Rhee knew how to attract private capital to the education sector which is never an attractive business area for investment. In retrospect our founding fathers knew the importance of raising the value of our only resource, human resources.

## All Brains are Created Equal

In America senior class teachers have to persuade parents of students with a good academic record to apply for university education, and if the parents find it difficult to pay for university tuition the teacher seeks scholarship opportunities. Good students usually find money for their tuition. This means most high school graduates do not seek for further education. In Germany at the end of high school education both student and teacher know in most cases who is going to university and who is going to professional school. There is hardly any conflict about this choice the student must make. The same scene in Korea is entirely different.

In most high school classes located in and around the city of Seoul, one hundred percent of the students plan to go to university. The teacher's role is to advise whether the student is good enough to try the entry examination to enter (1) the top three universities, (2) any of over 40 universities located within the boundary of metropolitan Seoul, (3) second and third tier universities located all around the country numbering close to two hundred, or (4) finally two-year professional colleges of nursing, machinery operation and repair, cooking, hairdressing, public health services etc.

The attitude of the typical parent is that there is nothing wrong with the brain of my child, as if all brains are created equal. If anything goes wrong, that must be the fault of the teacher, school or even the system. Since my investment in the education of my child is no less than that of other children, we must find ways to recover the investment one way or another. The Korean government had to adopt a uniform national examination system for college entry, that ranks the entire nationwide cohort of high school graduates every year, and educational consultants and teachers find the appropriate department and university that is just right for individual students. The system, that lasted over half century, was endlessly modified because of the demands of all sorts of parental groups, and became a set of inconsistent mutually contradictory rules and regulations that are still being modified. It is amazing how democracy sometimes can lift an aircraft carrier and put it on top of Mount Everest.

The Korean obsession for education puts learning above food and labor for many. That is an illogical paradox, but it is nevertheless a source of social energy that drove poverty away. The government didn't have to enact a bill mandating education, for people wanted to learn at all cost anyway. That's a paradox and waste of money. But the universal mandatory education system served more in providing equal opportunity of education to the poor. The ultimate question of whether the obsession with education made any positive contribution to the Korean development will be investigated in the chapter of Technology Nationalism.

## Private Sector Education Market

There is good education and better education but bad education is rare unless it focuses on an ideological indoctrination forcefully given for political purposes. But just as neighbors' gardens are always greener, in the education field parents either criticize and replace the teachers, blame the systems, or provide supplementary education to their children. We call that private education but in reality it is black market education. According to a study by the Ministry of Education,[9] the average payment of Korean families for private education for their children is invariably about 5% of their gross income regardless of their level of income. Annual total payment for private education in Korea amounts to a little less than half of Korea's public education budget. Since the education budget of Korea is just a little higher than the national defense budget, we spend more than half of the national defense budget on private education. It could easily be more than that for the black market data are always biased downward. For a country that is under constant alert for a possible invasion, this number shows how tough the private competitive education is.

Education is an economic service just as any economic good. But not all the economic goods and services are freely traded in the market. Some services like maintaining law and order, the national defense, and ensuring clean air are

---

[9] Yonhap News Service, 2021 03 09  by Jung, Hye Jin.

called public goods, because payment for them does not exclude those who did not pay or paid less from enjoying the same service. That is why we collect the fees for enjoying this special service through taxes using a different rule of sharing the burden of payment.

If this exclusivity rule is applicable, a good is called a market good and the law protects the buyer's right to monopolize the good. The trouble with education is that theoretically it is a market service and exclusivity can be applied. But when a whole nation thinks that education is important enough to make it a public service, then the government becomes the monopoly supplier of nationwide education and all the private and public schools become a network of subcontracted and franchised education suppliers. Most education is given free, including tertiary education in some cases, and the service is financed by taxes.

A monopoly supplier, the ministry of education in this case, can never satisfy the diverse needs and hopes of millions of buyers of education. A black market will form to fill the needs that are not served. That is *private education*. But even within the public education framework, good schools and bad schools pop up for many reasons including locating the school near a high income community, rich powerful alumni and donors, and teachers with extraordinary dedication to the outstanding achievements of students.

In ordinary and normal countries, these occasional hierarchical differentiations of school qualities are tolerated as natural. Not in Korea. For three quarters of a century parents of underachieving students supported by socialist political parties on the one hand, and parents of high achieving students supported by conservative politicians on the other, confronted each other. The former egalitarians with larger votes and under achieving children continued to legislate laws until the system no longer rewards excellence. The system ended up dismantling any hierarchy differentiation in educational quality. As a result, the parents of underachieving students now have to spend more money on black-market education. Shamelessly this is called the *policy of educational equalization*. The ultimate objective of the education system in Korea became not excellence but mediocrity. But even the parents who are leaders of the socialist party send their children to coaching colleges in search of excellence.

Egalitarianism in education in Korea creates deception by rewarding high payers more than high achievers.

The quality of Korean graduates however has proven to be fine. One way or other, graduates come to the employment market decently equipped with basic skills. But the process that the children must go through is, to me, totally irrational and paradoxical. The obsession with better education for children has become obscene, and after drilling the children for over 16 years from primary school to university, nearly all the applicants come to the job market with only insignificant differences in quality. This is because all the students went through the same furnace of madness called the Korean education system.

This achievement-oriented materialism that was manifested through a pathological obsession with education contributed to nation building through several channels. It supplied enough hard-working and smart laborers from the beginning of the developmental process. Over time the skilled workforce became the backbone of Korean middle class that gradually grew to be one of the most expensive workforces in the world. High performing elites sorted out through this net of examinations went to the best universities in the USA and Europe and became the agents of transplantation of world class education and research systems into Korea. The high standard of their research outputs surprises even the engineers of Apple, Google, and NASA. However, the best students became the government policymakers and corporate executives who, by the sheer force of market competition, had to survive the brutal international environment. The obsessive passion for education of Koreans seems to have worked.

Honestly I cannot recommend this Korean-style madness for education to poor countries planning to achieve prosperity in the near future. But unfortunately, I cannot think of any other way to achieve high quality research ability that surpasses Japan and challenges the USA. Without extraordinary demand for learning among the people and without extraordinary reinforcement for creativity in research and industry, becoming one of the richest economies of the world is unlikely. But learning breeds love of learning and raises demand for more learning as we have all experienced. One doesn't need an obsession with learning, but let's begin the first step of nation building with education.

# III. For Whom the Economy Grows

## Development Makes People Expensive

A country, just as an individual, faces many crossroads where it has to make a choice. The choice makes historical differences in economic and social consequences. Investing heavily in education even before the beginning of an economic take-off can turn out to be a disaster for a country, for the combination of *over education* producing a top-heavy structure comprised of an unhappy intellectual community and economic *stagnation* in entrenched poverty and corruption could easily create a chaos that leads to a communist revolution. The revolution would be led by the disgruntled radical intellectuals, whom Vladimir Lenin aptly called 'very useful fools.' Not all education raises human economic value. Each society differs in making use of the well-educated intellectuals.

The most outstanding consequence of any successful and sustained economic development transpires the fact that *people became expensive and valuable*. In fact, this is the purpose of any economic growth. If the economic development efforts of any country fail in making its people economically more valuable, if people are not regarded as more valuable by themselves and internationally, and if the government does not recognize the people as more valuable than before, the statistical economic growth that the government reports is very likely false. This is the case of Nong Min Gong workers, the rural industrial workers employed in the urban industrial centers of China where they cannot send their children to nearby schools. What they call *development* is merely an example of propaganda deception hiding the greed of the oligarchs.

The Nong Min Gong workers are not given residential rights to live near their work place, for the privilege of living in city is issued only to the permanent residents of the city by the communist party. The industrial migrant workers in the city are like mistreated foreign guest workers and they cannot send their children to city schools, or get the benefit of social medicine. In Korea children of visiting workers are subject to the mandatory education system and the universal medical insurance system. In China, Chinese workers from the countryside are excluded from such privilege. Their wage level is significantly lower than the urban residents and their human rights are disregarded. The CCP found these non-resident urban workers as being more obedient than the resident urban citizens. Any expression of dissatisfaction will cause deportation back to their country home. Chinese industrial corporations, both private and publicly-owned companies, and international investors jointly exploit the workers with cheap wages under the support of the communist party. This is identical to the comprador capitalism that exploited their compatriots for foreign capitalists. The Chines Communist Party provides a prime example of comprador capitalism.

The statistical economic growth of China has failed to raise the living standard of its people and their value. It is reported that at least 20% of the population still lives on 6 US dollars a day, which is well below the poverty line. Economic and social development is the process that helps people to achieve their self-respect by escaping pervasive poverty and realize their dreams by raising the economic value of their income and property. If economic growth does not raise people value, it is not development.

Usually poverty never stops men from aspiring and achieving high standard in arts, music, literature, and scholastic pursuits in the humanities and social sciences. But only a few with outstanding talent and luck achieve them. In a high-income society, higher income and property values enable more people to achieve their high cultural goals. Wealth raises the quality of life for most citizens. In China, unlike the people, the party does not seem to understand the meaning of high quality of life. Arts, music or drama should always be dedicated to the glorification of mother country and party leaders. Under this suppression of creativity and social exposé, it is only natural that the great talented individuals of China resort to illegal copying of foreign arts and products.[10]

This leads to a corollary to our trinity principle that only free democracy and market economy equipped with the system of private property ownership and freedom of

---

[10] Fan, Bing Bing and Lee, Bing Bing are two most beautiful and popular Chinese actresses with global fame, and both got so tired of and disgusted with the party intervention on their artistic activities as well as sexual insinuations that they decided to make homes in Korea

expression can *raise people value*. Even in poor and ancient agricultural autocratic societies, economies grew by producing more grain but never increased people value. It raised only the asset values of the rulers. But the true quality of people's lives rise only in societies where people have the right to raise the value of their income and property, and before that they should *own their property* first to raise the values. Korea demonstrated the *fallacy of common ownership* or denial of private property ownership in the name of the equal distribution of wealth.

## Asset Values and Value of the People

Human economic value in a country is often reflected in wages. People in a rich country dress differently, eat differently, and look differently compared to the people of poor countries. Higher wages are typically reflected in a higher per capita GDP. However, professional economists are generally under-informed about the role of the rising value of properties owned by average citizen of a country. The wealth effect of consumption is one good example in economic theory that takes into account the role played by the level of wealth in determining the cyclical changes of consumption but is rarely linked to the development of a society.

Economists have a very poor understanding of the peculiar interactive relationship between economic growth and changes in property values. They are particularly weak in explaining why wealth of the people rises in any country or any period of time. They are almost indifferent to the fact that higher value of the property owned by the people increases the value of the people.[11] Most economic theoreticians connect the rising value of private properties with inflation or speculation, without considering any positive effects. Readers will see later that the sufficient size of the middle class with the substantive market value of their assets, with equally large bank mortgage loans, is not only conducive to the maintenance of growth-oriented economic policies, but is also the source of the continuous supply of well-educated engineers and academics with overseas training, and it is highly supportive to the introduction of new technologies in their workplaces and homes. Korea

---

[11] Typical Japanese retirees with 200,000 dollars in life-time savings used to retire in Mauritius or Sri Lanka and lived like royalty before the 30 year long depression started..

is regarded as the test bed for new technologies by the so called platform companies such as Google, Amazon, and Apple. That means Korea has a highly responsive middle-class market that is sensitive to new technological experiments. Financial institutions such as banks regard the Korean middle class as being worthy of their trust and the value of their homes is high enough for mortgage loans.

In this chapter I will explain how poor families of penniless serfs started to turn themselves into middle class families, living in apartments with values at around one million US dollars, with their children now scattered all over the world working as business executives, engineers, professors, students, supervisors of construction sites overseeing workers from all over the Pacific and Indian Ocean countries. This process took about three generations and the trajectory of this change started with the unique paradox that brewed a pool of energy ready to explode. It shows that communism is not the only way to start a revolution that makes proletariats richer.

In August 1945 Korea was liberated from the brutal colonial rule of Japan and the entire country was filled with hope, a hope of instant freedom and prosperity for everybody. Rhetoric of the idealistic and socialistic intellectual leaders planted such illusions of instantaneous paradise in the people's mind. In the Northern half of the Peninsula, the Soviet military government organized the People's Council of the Chosun People's Republic in 1946, and Kim Ilsung was elected as the Chairman of that Council. In truth this Soviet Army major was nominated by the provisionary Soviet military government in Pyeongyang as the chairman of the People's Revolutionary Council. They knew that by setting up a local Revolutionary Council as quickly as possible, any demand by the American military government in Seoul to establish a unified government for the whole Korean Peninsula could be preempted. Entire peninsula was under one government for 14 centuries and the Soviet Army was invited, by President Franklin Roosevelt, into this territory to expedite the disarming the occupying Japanese forces. But the Soviets had a different plan. This was the inauguration of the North Korea as a separate country.

In the Southern half, one faction led by Mr. Gu Kim insisted on establishing one unified government ruling the entire Peninsula. This faction tried to negotiate with the

Kim's government, and, of course, Kim wanted the Southern half to be absorbed into his Pyeongyang government. After two-years of fruitless meetings, the US military government helped South Korean leaders organize the National Assembly of Korea that elected Dr. Syngman Rhee as the leader of South Korea's National Assembly. The assembly drafted and adopted the constitution, then held an election by which Rhee became the first president of the republic. Devilish authoritarian communist North became a pro-unification regime and free democratic South is blamed as a Separationist.

This Princeton PhD, who had a degree in political science, was a close associate of President Woodrow Wilson from his professorial days. As a jailed revolutionary republican at the last days of Lee Dynasty (1901),[12] he left immortal comments on communism: "No competition entails indolence, no freedom of speech entails corruption, no capitalist corporation entails poverty, no religion entails

---

12 *Japan Inside Out: The Challenge of Today*, by Syngman Rhee, Hardcover–September 15, 2017, originally published in 1941. Japan Inside Out was written as a warning to the United States about the dangers of Japanese totalitarianism. It was not until the attack on Pearl Harbor later that year that the insight of this work was appreciated. Nobel laureate Pearl Buck said that this is a book which Americans ought to read because it was written for them

immorality, and no sovereignty entails the disappearance of civilization." America, he saw, was rising from an isolated mediocre country to become a global leader by the power of industrial development under a free democratic market economy. He saw the formation and strengthening process of the American industrial middle class which participated in the process of American development as the main force and source of social energy.

The first major policy he declared after the inauguration was the mandatory education for the entire nation as we discussed previously. The second revolution he introduced was the Land Reform in 1949. More than 90% of the GDP was from agriculture in Korea.[13] More than 80% of the population resided in farmlands. To his painful realization, Dr. Rhee discovered that the nation was endowed with virtually no natural resources, and no industrial facilities were inherited from the Japanese rulers. Such facilities were mostly located in the Northern half. The electricity generation capacity of all of South Korea was a little over 35

---

[13] The world did not know the concept of GDP. It was not invented yet. The Statistical Commission of UN began the National Account Project in 1948 but the real GDP statistics were first published from 1968. Therefore, whatever we say about national products in days prior to this are retroactive estimates.

megawatts in capacity, when fully operational, and average income of the people was so low that there was virtually no domestic market for industrial goods. Total national exports amounted to a little over US$ 20 million, which consisted of tungsten and fishery exports. The only endowment was the people. With the mandatory education system, he forced the people to recognize their relative misery and woke them up from a thousand-year-old stupor of karmic poverty.

That was good motivation for massive changes. But one can do very little with empty hands. The national territory is about as large as the state of New Jersey, and 75% of the territory is uncultivable mountains, and that was all the resources we had then and now. Increasing agricultural productivity was inevitable but simply not enough. To raise the value of the people, he had to create a middle class with decent property ownership. He was a democratically elected president, and cannot follow the communist's government by confiscating all the land forcefully from the landed aristocrats and distributing it to the poor farmers free of charge. North Korea confiscated all the farmlands one year earlier and distributed the lands to regional People's Councils for collective farming. Private ownership of land is prohibited. Confiscating the bourgeois property for public ownership was the first item on their national agenda. Land reform is a communist tool, but to create a healthy middle class in which people own property, we needed to confiscate it first. A capitalist objective needed a communist tool.[14]

Throughout history, especially during the last days of the Lee Dynasty, the number of independent farmers possessing their own land declined monotonically due to persistent exploitations of local aristocrats and bureaucrats. Whenever a drought or flood occurred, farmers had to borrow grain from the rich to feed their family and pay the debt back in autumn. The interest rate was so high, many farmers failed to clear the debt and at the end of mounting debt, they gave up their small pieces of land they had inherited, and turned into tenant farmers or serfs. Rulers invented a system of labor conscription for national and local

---

[14] I used the words, *communist tool* loosely without rigor, for communists are split on the land redistribution issue. Achieving a farming without rents by confiscating land from rich landowners and distributing them to the poor tenants and serfs was enough for Karl Marx, but Stalin discovered that 85% of the population in the Soviet Union became property owners and he thought that is not the Communist Society he dreamed of. He took the policy of recollectivization of all the land and made the state the single landowner on behalf of the people.

infrastructure building projects on top of military conscription. In America dead voters voted sometimes according to Sen. Russell Long from Louisiana, and in old Korea dead fathers were called for conscription and the poor children served their terms, for the bureaucrats were never wrong; like computers fed with garbage. After hundreds of years repeating these extortions, independent farmers continuously lost their lands. At the time of the formation of the Republic of Korea, more than 90% of the farmers were tenants or serfs who received only 30% of the crops they produced.

In the process of planning the Korean land reform, a very interesting political twist was revealed to the public. Han Min Dang (the Korean Democratic Party-HMP), was the second largest party in the Korean National Assembly, and was comprised of returned Liberation Fighters and members of the provisional government that operated in China, mainly around Shanghai and Manchuria. Dr. Rhee was the choice of the US military government, and HMP became the opposition party against Rhee's Freedom Party. During the Japanese rule, educated children of rich landed families and scholars joined the Independence Movement. Some serfs and tenant farmers joined in guerrilla operations, but noble goals such as independence from foreign power were mostly beyond the concerns of serfs and tenants. If Japanese occupiers did not force labor without pay, or conscription of the girls for forced sex slavery, they would not have cared. These HMP members, the upper-class Bohemian romanticists of the 1920s and 30s were ideologically theoretical socialists, but they found themselves in a position to oppose the land reform of Dr. Rhee, for it is their lands that were being confiscated by the government. The recent three socialist governments of Kim, Dae Joong, Noh Muhyon, and Moon, Jae-in were voted into power because of the support of the Honam (South West) region, which is the richest agricultural base of HMP.

After lengthy confrontation, the government agreed to issue Land-Value Certificates to the land owners in exchange for the land taken and the land was sold to the farmers in 20-year installments. Land owners wanted something valuable for giving up their lands. By the Law of Land Reform (The 31st Law of the Republic) of June 1949, serfs and poor tenants became land owners and former land owners became owners of government-supported financial instruments with specified monetary values. The instruments were tradable in the market.[15] Tenants and serfs made contracts with the government who sold them the land at market price and the payment was arranged for twenty-year installments. Not everybody was happy but it was a decent solution to save the landlords and the tenants.

Mr. Bong Ahm Cho was the head of Korean Communist Party in Seoul. Both US military administration and Dr. Rhee had to honor the rights for freedom of thought. Kim Il Sung was the head of Korean Labor Party in Pyeongyang. And Mr. Cho was the head of Communist Party in Seoul. Dr. Rhee invited Mr. Cho to serve in his cabinet as the Minister of Agriculture and Forestry but Mr. Cho declined. Dr. Rhee further explained his plan for land reform, and then Mr. Cho gladly accepted the offer. Mr. Cho efficiently executed this revolutionary land reform, although it was not forced confiscation and free distribution of land in the typical communist style.

---

[15] There were only private financial markets that existed then and the certificates were usable as collateral for bank loans, that created long queues in front of trading banks. I cannot forget the endless visitors to our home, including the Buddhist priest who was the chairman of a Buddhist University Foundation, stayed many days eating only raw rice he carried, who wanted this collateral loan from the Industrial Bank where my father was a mere clerk.

The invasion of North Korea's communist army in the Korean War, which broke out just one year after the land reform, changed the results of the land reform dramatically. The war-oriented hyper-inflation in Korea virtually wiped out the nominal value of the land-value certificates issued in exchange for real land. The monetary value of the land certificates which government owed to the former land-owners became near zero. However, the same inflation reduced the farmers' liability to the government down to a meaningless level. In other words, Dr. Rhee ended up emulating the communist practice; forced confiscation of land and free distribution of them to farmers, without trying. Oh, the war did one more thing. Mr. Cho actively supported the occupying communist forces during the three-month occupation and after the return of the UN forces, he was executed for subversion.

## Evaporated Landed Class

Thus the Korean version of middle class was forcefully created regardless of how poor they were. Actually, in surveys taken from then and up to the 1997, when the Korean economy fell into a near-moratorium situation, 80% of respondents reported that they think they belonged to the middle class. The middle class to most Koreans is a concept of the relative importance of one individual or family in society, and it has nothing to do with the level of income. The importance of an individual or family is determined by the level of perceived participation in building a country, and most Koreans obviously think that they participate in major decisions that set the direction of the society. Many viewers and analysts of Korea wonder about the way Koreans express their dissatisfaction by demonstrating in the hundreds of thousands on city streets. The explanation is simple. They think if they do not resolve the problem, nobody else will do it for them. They think they are the owners of Korea.

At the start 80% of the Korean population was rural residents. They were the former serfs and landless tenants mentioned earlier. They were the same pool of human resources that supplied the industrial workers, construction workers in the Middle East, mining workers and medical nurses sent to Germany, the 40,000 combat soldiers sent to Vietnam, and the PhD candidates in the US, UK, German universities. If they received higher incomes in or outside of Korea, if they saved their income and invested in urban housing, if their investment value rose by several hundred times,[16] and if eventually a third of their property values rose over a million US dollars, then this is the grand visible evidence of economic development of Korea. They were the poor old Koreans, they became the main players in the drama of the economic growth, and they are the main beneficiaries of growth. They are indeed the main reason for the economic growth.

The main victim of this land reform is the former landed class. They lost their land and their economic base because of the war and following hyperinflation. Fortunately for them, virtually all of them possessed real estate in metropolitan centers where they had resided for several hundred years. But the basis of their wealth and power disappeared except for their human networks and tertiary education. Only a few of them started commercial activities, because such activities were against their instincts and pride, they despised commerce. Some of them proved to be

---

[16] Average housing price of Seoul rose by more than 1,000 times over the period from 1960- to 2020 and the GDP per capita rose in about 300 times during the same period.

resourceful enough to succeed in the manufacturing industry relying on their astute judgment. B.C.Lee (Samsung),
I.H. Koo (LG), D.B. Park (Dusan, Heavy equipment and
Desalination), W.J. Kim (Daewoo) are successful children
of former landed class parents. But most of them preferred
politics and academia and in about two generations all their
children disappeared in the oblivion of the massive middle
class. The children of former serfs and tenants by contrast,
such as, J.Y. Chung (Hyundai, former mechanic), J. H. Cho
(Hanjin, Korean Air and shipbuilding, former truck driver),
K. H. Shin (Lotte, Hotel and Petrochemical, former chew-
ing gum maker in Japan) are good examples of successful
children with a modest origin. We will examine more about
their role in Korean economic growth later.


## Evaporated National Capital


The preparation for take-off of the Korean economy
largely dominated the national agenda during the 1945 to
1961 period. Two major reforms, mandatory education reform and the land reform, built the basic structure for raising human values through education and private ownership

of land. Not many understood the magnitude of impact of the land redistribution. Land was the source and origin of food, tax, and power for states and sovereign for many millennia. Land ownership brought about many revolutions in the way food, wealth, tax burdens, and power are created. Human civilization, the concept of state, and protection of private property, even the wisdom of communitarian life came from the ownership of land. Hunters don't need to own land for hunting, but farmers do. For hunters the state is a necessary evil, while for farmers state is the protector of ownership of land and crops. Farmers had to invent state, law, and civilization.

Because of Korean land reform, the serfs and poor tenants became the proud owners of this basis of wealth and power. All they needed was to raise their productivity and to work harder and longer. But for their children the mandatory education system guaranteed a supply of useful knowledge and information that famers needed. Parents believed firmly that their children would not have to repeat the miserable lives they had lived in the past. These two events assured more than half of Korea's economic growth. Unlike the present poverty, their future depended entirely on the individual efforts and ingenuity. Never had the world been so fair and impartial to them.

It was not only the landed class and their assets that evaporated into the air. Korea's one and only source of national capital, capital embedded in land, which is called agricultural capital, disappeared too. At the beginning of industrialization, in Europe and other parts of the world, owners of large tracts of land raised the capital they needed for industrial investment by offering their land as collateral. The agricultural capital naturally turned into industrial capital and the new industrial class is created from among the old agricultural capitalists. But in Korea, all the farming land was split into small pieces and the poor farmers didn't have enough income for any savings, let alone investments in new industries. The government came up with the idea of issuing industrial bonds but the market response was miserable. Korea had to start its industrialization by *borrowing*. But who would lend capital to a small and war-torn country? For any country planning for a rapid development, it is imperative that one should preserve the capital base of traditional land ownership. All countries without exception have landed class and their property value is the key to industrialization. It is not easy to believe that the greedy detested landed class has a positive role to play in the modernization of a nation, but believe me without them, the difficulty of economic development doubles.

Economies grow without communist-style land reforms and without millions of wealthy middle-class families. The world is full of examples where alternating gyrations between socialist governments and conservative governments stagnated the economy over time. The social cost related to the massive-scale nationalization of major industries, and then the rush to privatization of them can easily wipe out any gains of past growth. The United Kingdom suffered from this gyration more than any advanced industrial country. If you want continuous and cumulative economic growth, under a democratic system, you need strong political support from a stable middle class large enough to dominate the electoral booth. Only a strong and stable middle class can prevent political ideologues from using our country and system as their ideological testing laboratories.

The middle class of any country, however, is an ambivalent bunch that sometimes thinks that they are the beneficiaries of economic growth and support the conservative cause of strong growth, and sometimes think that they are the victims of distorted growth and distribution. Korea, as we will see in subsequent chapters, did not try to raise a strong and prosperous middle class, but we did not try to stop them either from trying their best in building their asset bases. We did not particularly employ any specific *incomes policies* but left the market to determine relative income distributions. However, we did encourage our middle class to compete with each other in building their asset bases by opening a wide range of opportunities in urban redevelopment projects and making a massive amount of financial resources for mortgage loans available.

# IV. Indefensible Country

## Importance of Korea, Two Opposing Views

South Korea is tactically indefensible. It is connected to the Asian main land through the demilitarized zone shared with the North Korea, whose national goal is to invade the South and force unification with nuclear threats or more. South Korea is surrounded by seas on three sides, two of which are shared with Japan and China. Japan never hides its national hostility and contempt for Korea, and the two countries are engaged in many disputes with each other, real or deliberately created.

Mr. Xi, Jinping, the supreme leader of China publicly declared that Korea was part of China in the past, and some four hundred thousand military force of the Peoples Liberation Army invaded Korea during the Korean War in 1950 to fight against the UN military forces and the US army in particular. Moreover, by the order of the CCP, Chinese historians just completed an academic *operation* which describes ancient Korean history as a part of ancient Chinese history. This is their style of preparing for the military incorporation of North Korea.

The Soviet Union became the second most powerful nation in the world after the WWII[17] and took on the goal of communizing the entire world as a national objective, and this is considered to be more important than the economic progress of its people. The Soviet Union successfully assisted the Chinese Communist Party in defeating the Kuo Min Dang army and unifing the entire China mainland. The Soviets called this endeavor Comintern, an abbreviation of the Communist International Movement that helped communist parties all over the world, particularly in the newly independent states of Asia and Africa, in their subversive activities and propaganda. The CCP succeeded in this task and made its embassies and local organizations such as Confucius Institutes as a propaganda apparatus for this cause. Many suspects that the One Road-One Belt

---

[17] The Soviet Union after WWII rapidly grew in strength particularly in nuclear weapons, rockets, and in the space race. In some sector such as the space industry its strength surpassed the USA sometime in the late 1950s.

proposition by China is a sophisticated extension and manifestation of the latent subversive goals of communism.

From the point of view of the Soviets, South Korea originally was a defenseless but significant piece of land at the tip of the Eurasian Continent that could open the entire Pacific Ocean to the Soviet Navy with access to unfreezing seaports with the added bonus of threatening the Japan Archipelago which the US Navy protected. The West Pacific defense line implemented in 1949 by Mr. Dean Acheson, the US Secretary of State, notably excluded the Korean Peninsula. Stalin took that as an invitation for invasion and instigated North Korea to invade South Korea providing offensive weapons and support including tanks, artillery, and pilots. The exclusion of the Korean Peninsula from this defense line shows how insignificant South Korea was from the American point of view.

The paradox is that the US government ended up with over 50,000 US military personnel killed in action and over 300 thousand injured in a three-year-long war in defending this insignificant terrain.[18] Two days after the invasion start-

---

[18] It is reported that at the news of the North Korean invasion young Billy Graham called

ed, the Joint Security Council of the United Nations held a special meeting to discuss the issue of creating a UN Military Force to help defend South Korea from the communist invasion. After lengthy and chaotic debates, at the moment of voting, the loquacious Mr. Vishinski, the Soviet ambassador to the UN, vacated his seat and lost his chance to use his veto power.[19] Thus the UN Peace Force was created and over 70 countries from all over the world rose to help; 16 of them sent actual military units to fight and others sent economic, medical and military aid, all to save this *useless* land of Asia.

The Republic of Korea, which shrank to the size of Queens Island at the darkest hours of the war, maintained its independence and started to rebuild itself in 1953. It is now the 8th largest economy in the world,[20] and it has the

president Harry Truman at 4.00 am in the morning demanding that the US troops stationed in Japan be sent immediately to Korea to defend this land, and Mr. Truman did. Korea was a Christian country more than any other Asia country.

[19] According to the Russian government's confidential documents released after the fall of the Soviet Union, Stalin instructed Vishinski to deliberately abstain from voting in order to draw the material-rich USA and manpower-rich China to engage in a prolonged conflict until they drained themselves. That would have made the Soviets the supreme power of the world. But the American people were war-fatigued, and this forced them to agree to an armistice three years afterward.

[20] Due to the negative growth of the real GDP caused by the coronavirus pandemic Russia, India and Italy dropped behind Korea.

6th most powerful military force after the USA, Russia, China, India, and, Japan[21] according to the reports of SIPRI (Stockholm International Peace Research Institute). It has taken about 70 years. In 1953, when the war ended, Korea was and still is indefensible in 2021. Three of the above powers that surround South Korea are either visibly or potentially hostile, and the nearest neighbor, nuclear-powered North Korea, still makes controlling South Korea its national reason for existence. So the existence of South Korea is both a paradox and a miracle.

## US-Korea Military Alliance and Korean Insecurity

In 1953 to President Syngman Rhee and all Korean people, nothing was more certain than the simple fact that so long as the North Korean communist government is left alive, the Korean Peninsula will never be peaceful. The Pyongyang regime was at its weakest, ready to be extin-

---

[21] Korea independently developed offensive missiles with a range of 6000km, and that covers the entire territory of Japan, and Japan has a superior navy but inadequate missile interception ability. Korea is capable of designing world's only nuclear SMR (small modular reactor).

guished at a stroke by the superior military of the UN forces.

North Korea started the war with the expectation that the war would last half a year at most. There was no way Kim, Il Sung would have understood the intention of Stalin who wanted a war of attrition between the USA and China. North Korea was not prepared to sustain three-year long conflict and neither China nor the Soviet Union offered economic aid. It was the historic chance for achieving lasting peace on this Peninsula through unification. But Koreans don't elect the US president, and Americans were tired of the war that seemed to drag on in a remote unknown place. Mr. Dwight Eisenhower, the president-elect took the popular option – stopping the massive killing, and leaving the job of defending Korea to Koreans and the US *military-industrial complex*, the words he used first.

Dr. Rhee did his best to obstruct the joint armistice meeting at Pan Mun Jum, by not appointing a South Korean representative to attend. Massive civic parades in opposition to the cease fire were staged by the government. He released nearly 100 thousand POWs by widely opening the gates of prison camps on Koje Island in order to give the North Korean prisoners a chance to escape and hide in nearby houses of South Korean families. If the armistice was implemented they were bound to be sent back to North Korea in exchange for the POWs held by the other side. More than 95% of them did not want to go back to the North. Most of Chinese prisoners did not escape and were sent back to China. But that did not stop the armistice.

As a condition for South Korea to refrain from interfering with and obstructing the armistice negotiation between the USA and China plus North Korea, Dr. Rhee demanded and received the gift of the Joint Security Treaty between the USA and the Republic of Korea. This created the legal basis for US troops to remain in Korea and the foundation for 68 years of cease-fire. Presently, US taxpayers wonder why America should pay for the defense of South Korea. In the 1950s and 1960s when China was militarily and economically insignificant, this was a valid question, but hardly anyone asked, for the American economy was so powerful and overwhelming that it could easily afford the burden. In the 70s and 80s when the US federal budget deficit roughly matched its trade deficits and imported crude-oil bill, the US was preoccupied with (1) managing the stability of crude oil importation and securing routes of oil transportation, (2) flirting with China for an alliance against the common Soviet the threats, and (3) controlling selfish allies who had no hesitation in adopting mercantile policies in trade and exchange rate distortions against US interests. Audacious and almost impudent pressures against the Soviets by President Reagan with Star War technology for missile interception resolved the four-decade-old Soviet problem by causing the Soviet Union to dismantle.

That raised new hope for the West in *China opportunities*. Western politicians and intellectuals had no doubt that economic advancement in China with its market economy would bring in *political development*, meaning liberal politics and democratic progress in China. Western corporations rushed to capture the world's largest market before others did. But this optimism soon turned into an unexpected new reality – a *China threat*. The three decades beginning in 1990 were the golden ages for China and brought the *China dream* within sight as an achievable goal but harsh domestic politics returned China back to the pre-Deng Shao Ping period.

The problem is that this China dream is based on Sino-centrism and it directly collides with the self-determination of all other countries in the world. China's One Road and One Belt turned out to be a smarter version of 19th-century imperialism, and it was designed to collide with the national interests of smaller countries. This anachronistic and blunt pursuit of national egoism is revealed to be against the civilized world, and global peace and freedom. Illegal occupation of the South China Sea in disregard of the International Court Decision, the threat of military invasion of Taiwan, and building a naval armada larger than the US Navy eclipsed the question of US cost of defending Korea.

The role of multinational military forces deployed in the East Asian region is to deter China's military from taking any rash actions. The Chinese military knows that they cannot defeat US forces although they can cause some damage. China cannot afford military conflict in North East Asia, especially at this difficult time. Maintaining stability in the region is the best option for them. Therefore, US ground forces has the limited role of keeping Kim's army from breaking the delicate military equilibrium in the region. That's cheaper defense policy than fighting.

# Defense of South Korea as a Factor of Economic Growth

In this modern world of high-tech weapons, winning a war is frequently less of an object than preventing a war. The cost of winning is usually far too expensive. Preventing war is equivalent to maintaining a security equilibrium which means maintaining the level of fire and manpower on both sides at an equal level so that no party can expect outright victory. Since Hiroshima and Nagasaki, the world has successfully kept this rule and prevented war on a global scale. In this regard the fact that there was no hot war on the Korean Peninsula for 70 years is proof that the military balance was well kept here. But that was not easy when the US government continuously tried to break the balance in ways that give a tactical advantage to our enemies.

Korea went through a very peculiar experience that confirmed their traditional wisdom that says *Don't trust Americans*. The first shock was given by President F. Roosevelt by agreeing to draw a line at the 38th parallel and invited Soviet ground forces as occupying forces. But the Soviet Union was in a non-invasion agreement with Japan until two weeks before the Hiroshima bombing. They changed only after the Hiroshima bombing. America didn't need Stalin who didn't want to fight against Japan. Korea didn't have to be divided. The second shock was given by Dean Acheson, the Secretary of State for President Truman, who excluded the Korean Peninsula from the West Pacific defense line of US forces from communist invasion and publicly announced it. If America wanted to ditch Korea, they could have done that quietly, but they announced it publicly. We didn't know that America never publicly committed to the defense of democratic countries from communist invasion, we just assumed that. And we were wrong.

The third time that we experienced American betrayal is when Jimmy Carter was elected to the presidency with his policies to withdraw US forces from Korea. President Nixon announced the policy of US Forces withdrawal first, but Carter gave higher priority and commitment to it. Under global stagflation after the first oil shock, the US government budget deficits, and its trade deficits, which were getting close to 5% of the GDP, the US government badly needed to reduce the budget deficit. That will create a huge gap in the regional military balance. This time we were ready to take action to restore the balance. Korea has been running a primitive defense industry program since the late 60s in the name of the *lightning policy* because a Korean company developed an automatic rifle in 40 days starting from zero. Korea started to add the heavy, mechanical, chemical, and electronic industries to our portfolio of light consumer goods industries.

In retrospect, I think we should be thankful to Mr. Acheson and Stalin for turning on the key for Korean modernization by starting the Korean War, and to Mr. Carter for sending us the early warning that we should be militarily independent to survive in the tough neighborhood of Japan, Russian, North Korea, and China. These two leaders took out the hidden desperation of Koreans, and such desperation proved the strongest source of motivation for survival, namely development.

It is, in truth, post-traumatic stress that all Koreans suffered during most of our developmental stages, and that stress characterized the peculiar Korean behavior and history. I am not talking about the rushing lifestyle of individual Koreans which is known as Bali Bali culture. When a whole society suffers from this syndrome, unique histories are created like the post-WWI nihilism of Weimar Germany. The extraordinary financial burden imposed on Germany gave birth to the hyperinflation that the world cannot forget and brewed Nazism underneath.

In Korea, this same syndrome crushed the traditional communitarian disdain on wealth and implanted a new value and respect to egoistic materialism. But it gave stronger side effects by planting a deep-rooted anti-communism, that entailed (1) generous tolerance to the authoritarian governing by the military junta, (2) a frenzy rush to economic growth in competition vis a vis North Korea, and (3) nationwide support to the building of an independent defense capability that required a viable weapons industry. National Defense Surtax garnered the resources for creating weapons industries.

The ruling police officers and their followers tortured students in ways not tolerated in a normal democratic society but Korea was not a normal democratic country at the beginning. This authoritarian government successfully triggered the flame of economic growth and social reformation and it is still burning furiously. But the militant unions and radical students had different priorities. Amazingly the same conflict is still going on strong with one difference that the ambivalent center is widening.

Unusually high national aspiration for economic growth succeeded in taming down the student and labor activism and turned even the union members into investors in stocks and residents. This regimental society continued until the early 1980s when political and intellectual elites and grass-root activists tacitly agreed that it is time to go democratic.

Korea is not large enough to build a viable defense in-dustry, not to speak of the lack of advanced high technolo-gies that modern weapons demand. During the 50 years since the beginning of mechanical and electronic indus-tries, Korea's technology matured enough to develop some of its own high-tech weapons, and the world suddenly en-countered a shortage of American weapons supply capacity due to a prolonged war in Ukraine. And the complacent Europeans slowly and steadily closed down their weapons industry which may take over ten years to restore. To ev-erybody's surprise including Koreans, Korea became the only country that can fill this gap.

Needless to say, the lesson from the Korean experience shouldn't be that one should start a war with neighbors. Jealousy on a national scale of wealthy neighbors could do the trick and smart politicians all over the world use *Hate-Your-Neighbor* campaigns. The impact naturally is very limited. But tension always helps. In building a foundation for takeoff, intensification of the collective energy of the society to escape poverty caused by a local war proved powerful, and the suffocating stagnation entrenched by the greedy rulers and ignorant serfs demanded a shock treatment to shatter the old culture.

# V. The Story of Taking Off

## From Chaos to Take-Off

At the beginning, when Korea started, democracy was an unfamiliar experiment for the Korean intellectuals because under the old Korean system, intellectuals were equal to aristocracy or at least bureaucracy and accountability by ordinary people, the subordinates, was natural. But *accountability to subordinates* and the people by the superiors was a very new concept and very uncomfortable. But accountability to the subordinates is the central principle of democracy. During this period, accountability to the people that was enforced by the active free press was, although theoretically understandable, mostly disregarded, and the press could easily be bribed then.[22] The system quickly

---

22 Chosun Ilbo and Dong A Ilbo are two of the oldest and stubbornly independent daily newspapers with largest circulations in Korea. Their editorial bias to free democracy and national independence is well known and invited unbearable pressures from Japanese government, military governments and socialist governments who value human liberty less than most Koreans. To fight against the bribery of their reporters Chosun Ilbo raised

turned into one of no accountability. Democracy turned into a system of unlimited freedom without supervision. As a result political and bureaucratic corruption and illegal practices like extortions and embezzlement became overt and routine in Korea.

Japan and China now seem to be situated right at this point of history. Citizens should not criticize or resist the government policies and the staffs of companies should not question decisions made by corporate superiors in these countries even today. Japanese people call such behavior as a restraint for the social harmony but when an entire nation places social harmony above the social justice, the system falls by corruption. They express their discontent by low turnout on election days but that prevents reforms. Serious large scale corruption by politicians is occasionally exposed but the prosecutors and media jointly love to cover it up. And people proudly express their dissatisfaction by turning their face away, saying that they are not interested in politics. Somebody must tell them that that is called cowardice and there is nothing to be proud of it. Martin Luther King

---

salaries and expense account of its staffs to one of the highest in Korea including globally prosperous Korean corporations during the last days of military government.

called that silence a terror.

Confucian demand for respect for the king, teacher, and father directly contradicts the dictum of accountability to subordinates. The central concept of Confucianism comes from *li* in Chinese and *Ye* in Korean. It defines the human relationship in vertical order and assigns roles and attitudes of every individual of the society in an orderly ranking; *King, Teacher, Father, and Friend.* It is wise statecraft for the days when rule by law had not been invented yet. In this system accountability to subordinates or people was a blasphemy. Inefficiency and bribery permeated deep into the corporate sector and various institutions, for leaders failed to make themselves accountable to the people.

But this situation was interrupted by the North Korean and Chinese invasion in 1950 that lasted for three years and devastated the entire Peninsula. I would not get into the debate of who invaded first because Stalin confessed that he is the villain. Seven years from Armistice to the fall of government (1960) was a period of struggle against the post-Korean war hyperinflation and balancing the national budget, which requires raising taxable income or economic growth.[23] As soon as the goal came into view in 1961, US economic aid ceased suddenly. The *student revolution* followed and President Rhee resigned.[24]

But in the middle of the chaotic convolution of numerous political parties, corrupt bureaucracy, military and uncontrollable inflation, the poor but dedicated teachers diligently educated their children all around the country and laid a decent foundation for future economic growth. Korea was reaching the end of the L-shaped curve staying at the bottom waiting for a shock to jump start the economic growth that is called Take-Off. And it came in the form of harsh military ruling.

An American economic historian, Walter W. Rostow, published a book called "The Stages of Economic Growth" in 1960.[25] He argued that economic modernization occurs in

---

[23] Most governments including Japan and USA try to balance their budgets. If one cannot reduce spending, the only way left is to raise tax. Raising tax without raising taxable income, namely economic growth, is a political suicide under democracy. Japan gave up balancing its  budget and keeps on borrowing. Everybody is watching how far Japan can continue this.

[24] This author was a member of the student mob as a senior class member. I lost two friends, one a close classmate, in this revolution.

[25] "The Stages of Economic Growth–A Non-Communist Manifesto", Cambridge University Press, 1960 by Walter Whitman Rostow

five basic stages; traditional society, preconditions for take-off, take-off, drive to maturity, and mass consumption. This taxonomy quickly became a standard conceptual framework with which students of economic and social development used to effectively communicate with each other.

Using his jargon Korea finished laying the groundwork for take-off by (1) building the land-owning middle class from former serfs and uneducated tenant farmers who comprised 80% of the total population, (2) forcefully educating them to prepare for further training for advanced farming, manufacturing skills, using modern equipment, and international trading, and convincing them that in the world they are entering, continued education is the only way to survive, and (3) instilling massive energy of self-confidence in them for self-improvement, or the famous *can do spirit* that they acquired through the survival from the battlegrounds by watching the deaths of their friends and family members in their arms or just a meter or two away.

Economic take-off without building an intelligent middle class is not impossible but it will not sustain the growth. The majority of the population who feels that they are left out of the growth experience will turn the society into something like the typical Latin American countries with constant gyration between stagnation and occasional growth. The take-off supported by an uneducated labor force will slowly sink back, for the manufacturing process that requires continuous retraining of the workforce cannot survive. As average wages rise by the take-off, foreign companies will move away to other cheap-wage countries. To uneducated workers studying is far more painful than low wages. To the workforce that believes that they belong to the middle class, continuous education was required to remain in the same class, That is a tremendous motivation for studying new tricks. And in the end without the help of these well-experienced technicians no scientist can even dream of creating new products and samples.

The strong motivation of the people for economic growth is one of the fundamental building blocks for continuous economic growth. In this sense Korea was ready for a take-off in people, motivation, self-confidence, education, and even healthy dose of greed. The growth machine of Korea was ready to take-off and the record shows that once it took off, it never stopped flying upward.

# Reluctant Entrepreneurs

If the goal of individual members of a company coincides with the goals of companies where they work, and the common goals of the nation where the people and companies are located coincide with each other, miracles can happen. Sometimes in the history of every country, this triangular wave occurs. That is the best time for a take-off. Korean people were charged with energy to escape poverty, and the new military government was ambitious for quick achievement of economic growth. But we found a critical missing link in the Korean economy; an energetic, innovative and active corporate sector. People wanted economic growth, and the government wanted the same. But there were only a few insignificant companies who had to carry out the roles of investment, production. and export.

For seven years after the cease fire, Korea was fully engaged in recovering from the scars and wounds of the war. People were ready to do anything to escape the hunger and poverty of the war, but more than 80% of the GDP came from the agricultural sector and fisheries. Neither the government nor the farmers knew what to do with an economy which did not have a single plant of urea fertilizer. The early 1960s was the turning point of Korean history, and it marked the end of the probationary period of Korea, which gave it the time for creating a nation, surviving through a devastating war, and recovering from the wounds of the war.

The publicly declared object of the military coup of 1961 transpired into a genuine social and economic revolution, which is summed up in the series of *Five Year Economic and Social Plans*, and their implementation. In this process, the generals found out to their surprise that the most critical bottleneck in the economic development effort was in the shortage of good entrepreneurs and a vibrant corporate sector. Right after the coup, generals arrested some 30 Korean business men for anti-social activity such as *'profit seeking'*[26] by manipulating the market price of essential consumer goods such as rice and flour. They called it speculation. However, the same activity in mature market economies is called as futures trading; namely selling when the price is high (shorting) and buying when the price is low (going long). Both the media and the public applauded

---

[26] Yes, profit seeking. That was the sin. Contempt and disparaging the positive role of the wealth-seeking class was still alive strong in the minds of military officers.

this *socially just act* of the young officers. It never came to their mind that futures trading reduce the amplitude of the price fluctuations and this *speculation* continues until there is no more profit to be made.

Theoretically aggregation of uncoordinated individual greed ends up with optimal price equilibrium and any digression from it automatically stabilizes back to the equilibrium over time. That is the beauty of the free market which Adam Smith, the father of modern economics discovered. But that was a mere theory to the generals. Besides, as Smith admitted, this theory applies only to a stable, free, and prosperous world in peace. That is another way of saying when our trinity of developmental goals is already achieved, market economy brings growth through optimization. That is laissez-faire.

After having been briefed about the first five year plan, Gen. Park, the head of the coup discovered the plan was only a series of investment projects that needed companies that invest, and entrepreneurs to manage them. The general invited Mr. Byung Chul Lee, the founder of Samsung and asked for help. The result was the immediate release of the jailed businessmen and the establishment of new organization called the Federation of the Korean Industries (FKI). Most of the businessmen were merchants of various goods but the concept of a *modern corporation* was new to them. Some of them ran textile plants or coal mines but none of them were exposed to international trade. They were good only at selective risk-taking for good returns.

The responsibility of the burden of investment was allocated to the businessmen, and they were not happy. They were mere merchants of rice, coal, bicycles, automobile repairs, and small scale manufacturers of fabrics. None of them had access to the technology needed to set up a plant for manufacturing the products required. Clearly it was a short cut that would cause the loss of all of their capital that was woefully meager compared to the money needed to construct the required plants at a scale large enough to lower the product costs to international level. But their lives were more important than the small amount of capital they might lose. And the reluctant Korean entrepreneurs complied to the order of the military government.

Development economists are very uncomfortable with

this approach of starting with large scale investment to secure internationally competitive low product cost. They came up with a long list of reasons that such an approach was highly unlikely to succeed and could cause the waste of the valuable capital. If a country can build and operate a plant of exportable products in an internationally competitive scale, it is not a poor developing country, they would say. In order to reduce the risk, it was strongly advised by the economists of financial institutions to reduce the scales of investment down to a *manageable level.*

If a poor country follows this advice and aims at the domestic markets only, a business will fail quickly, because the domestic market is severely limited as the majority of the consumers cannot afford to buy much of the newly manufactured goods. Economists then proudly write their discovery of the *vicious circle of poverty,* explaining why poor countries can never join the rich countries' club. They did not know that the entrepreneurs who invested the entire sums of their thousand-year old family capital could create the miracle of survival. Their successes were more frequent than expected. Korean government subsidized its export industries and it was pre-WTO days. Generals badly needed success stories of export-oriented growth.

China has set up a new standard of exclusively subsidizing Chinese companies on an unprecedented scale. Subsidy to Chinese companies should have been retaliated by countervailing tariffs under the WTO frame work, but Mr. Biden chose to subsidize American companies instead. For 30 years America gladly exported its jobs to China, now it is forcefully importing jobs back from China and the rest of the world. Friendly allies suddenly became collateral victims in this Sino-American job war. Everybody thought that MAGA Trumpians are Isolationist, while Democrats and Globalists care interests of alliances more. One sage once said to me, 'Who says the world is rational?'

The Korean government assigned two to three contenders to each industry thus the future Korean oligopolies, called Jaebol, were born. The government had to milk-feed them by doing everything from allocating land for plant locations, enticing American and Japanese companies to help the Korean counterparts, forcing domestic banks to lend running capital to them, providing financial guarantees to international banks for imports of facilities and raw materials as well as giving out various other material incentives. I make these remarks casually but this is precisely the very basic steps for poor countries to industrialize from scratch. In fact the rest of this book is devoted mainly to describing the hardships and success stories in each of the above tasks that Korea had to resolve.

Thus by this addition of a set of reluctant entrepreneurs in the march for an economic take-off, the missing part of the triangular tidal wave was arbitrarily created. The Korean economy was ready for a successful take off and the first five–year economic plan was the ignition trigger. The rest of the story is well-known history and repetition of it will sound like government propaganda. But the process of creating the wealth of a nation should continue at least three generations to reach a stable mass prosperity.

Korean people suffer from xenophobia and Korean companies lacked international competitiveness and experience. Historically whatever came from across the sea was always destructive, disastrous, and dangerous to Koreans. Finally, Koreans were liberated from painful foreign exploitation, and *being left alone* was the sweetest dream for

Koreans. But Koreans didn't realize that their future lied out there; in the global market. One of the most important gains made during the first two five–year development plans was the successful establishment of the General Trading Companies (GTC) called the *Jonghap Sangsa* in Korea. Samsung Group registered the first GTC and total 10 groups of companies got the license for GTC.

The manufacturing companies were too small to open foreign offices, too poor to hire experienced international staff, and too inexperienced to develop overseas markets. Korea needed a well-organized international commercial window to represent all the small producers of exportable goods produced in Korea at a reasonable cost. We found the answer in the general trading company. This type of company does not produce any goods therefore it cannot compete against its client-supplier companies.[27] Each GTC created and operated a vast international network of import/export offices located typically in over 60 cities of 30 countries. Its short-term target was to find and expand markets for Ko-

---

[27] Japanese Sogo Shosa preceded our GTC but the Japanese version produces goods and is active in acquiring small producers, hence the number of subsidiaries grew to several hundreds. Korean version is more focused on assisting small domestic producers to export. In the end Korean GTCs were allowed to acquire production units overseas especially in resource development industries.

rean supplier-client's products including the arrangements for the after-services following exports. But their long term goal was to create stable credit lines from the international financing institutes for bigger future projects.

The service fees the GTC collected from the Korean producers they represented were less than 1% if not zero, and the GTCs made their bread and butter mainly from the generous excess import quota and access to the ever-scarce foreign exchange that the government allocated. Since this import quota was allocated in proportion to the size of exports the GTCs successfully assisted, all the major and medium size GTCs diligently competed for more exports. The dollar value of sales, not the profit, was the national as well as the corporate goal for Korea during most of the pre-crisis period. The crisis of 1997 woke us up to the cold fact that more sales and borrowing, with low or no profit, is the shortcut to bankruptcy.

To the public and government, the rapid rise in export volume adds to the GDP growth rate and therefore coincides with the goal of the country, whereas profit only adds to the wealth of the company. Various subsidies and government awards were allocated in proportion to the rise in export volumes. At 12 noon, December 31 of every year, the director and staffs of the computer center of the National Customs Office had to hide to escape from the pressure of the GTC staffs who wanted to register the last export letter of credit documents that will make their company the number one exporter of the year.

GTC offices in London, Paris, and New York were able to detect the changes in market trends early enough to prepare the Korean garment-producing clients for early access to new designs and critical fabrics. For this purpose, some GTCs such as Samsung Co. Ltd, where this author served as EVP, acquired local brands in Paris and New York together with Korean garment makers.

One of the major contributions made by GTCs was centralizing the vast procurement task brought up by Korean construction companies as they won biddings of major engineering and construction projects in the Middle East after the first oil crisis. Our London office, for instance, had to acquire a sufficient amount of steel bars, cement, a supply of water, glass products, heavy equipment, trucks, buses, and entire life-supporting items for dormitories, cooks, guards, design engineers, and an entire labor force. For companies with projects in multiple locations, the task was more complex. Our New York office imported Turkish steel products to serve the American market for instance. Centralizing such produrement activities raised the price advantage of pooled purchases. This operation created a powerful base upon which decent credit lines were established. In other words, the 1960s textile and shoe manufacturers of Korea prepared themselves for international project management in the heavy-mechanical-electronic industries in the 1970s.

## Import Substitution is Market Augmenting[28]

Suppose China can produce smartphones and chips *relatively* cheaper than other countries in the world. In trade theories of economics, this relativity is defined in most peculiar way. Suppose both China and Korea produce phones and chips. If China's cost advantage is greater in

---

[28] This awkward expression is a jargon from Economics. Like higher degree of freedom in statistics, market augmenting is one of the criteria for deciding good from bad.

phones than in chips over Korea, China should produce only phones and Korea should produce only chips. All the other countries should select a product where it is most competitive disregarding China. The total expenditure spent in making the smartphones and other products in the world will be at the lowest. The Chinese would be happier because more Chinese would be employed and Koreans, Americans, and Europeans would be happier because they would get their smartphones at a cheaper price. Do you believe this theory?

If all the western workers are well trained in IT, Semi-conductors, or Aerospace industries, they can be re-employed in *new* industries, and China will concentrate on producing only smartphones for a very long time to come. But this is an unreal condition. Many western workers are not technically prepared for re-education and new employment, and China will never continue to concentrate only on making smartphones. I am happy that the above caricature did not actually happen because the economic policymakers are smarter than David Ricardo, the British economist who invented the theory of comparative advantage.

Most importantly, this theory of comparative advantage holds true only when time has stopped and no further new technology appears on the horizon. That is why in developmental economics there should be no room for this theory. Economic development is a process of *introducing new industries and technologies* into third-world countries and making the relevant companies strong enough to survive in the highly competitive international markets. That is a *dynamic restructuring of the existing comparative advantage structures* of many mature products presently produced in advanced manufacturing countries.

This global adjustment is a genuine market augmenting process. When a poor country hosts a new industry, there will be a large reduction in imports. The fact that the country imports any good in a large volume testifies that it has a large domestic need and market for that product. Import substitution is the answer to the question, 'Where to start.' If you are an agricultural exporter such as Uzbekistan, chances are your big ticket import item is machines related to cotton farming, harvesting, and manufacturing cotton fabrics and textiles. You can choose to increase cotton production by better farming, better irrigation, and proper use of fertilizers. But its growth contribution is limited by the amount of farmland and the size of the labor force. If, however, many poor countries produce spinning machines and the rich country produces the weaving machines, then the new global system of cotton textile industry will experience a genuine income explosion and market augmenting result.

For the old agricultural machine industry of rich country, they have to diversify into more sophisticated machines for cotton textiles or polyester and nylon industries with higher efficiency. With the advanced technology of agricultural machinery they can invent cheaper tractors and combines for the small farmers all over the world. They can subcontract hundreds of local assemblers to produce and market final machine products in their locality. Mother company will supply the engines and transmissions in much larger volumes. This way the import substitution of one country can lead to income and market augmentation in many countries with new products and technologies.

Since there are very few cotton growers in the world, cotton-growing poor countries will want to become the cotton machine suppliers and they will ask to share the machine technology. They will eventually localize the production and improve on the machine designs. This is what all the great capital goods importers of the world do. It is nearly impossible to substitute imports of iron ore and coal, but machines can be substituted by local products. Building an *import substitution industry* is the best starting point. That solves the big question of *where to start*.

## Changes in Farm Sector

Agriculture is not one of the leading sectors of Korea. Korean economic development is a drama that took three generations in which the children of the free farmers left the farm sector in steady streams until the farm sector was left with a very aged population with less than a 5% contribution to GDP. The urban industrial sectors were built by these educated children who left home. During every long holiday based on folk culture (A long holiday means 5 days in Korea.) these children drive their cars with grandchildren and spend 10 hours covering distances that normally take 2 to 3 hours. The grandparents are very proud that their children have become successful urban workers and engineers with international experience. Grandparents are happy that their early investment in the education of their children has brought satisfactory returns.

The Korean farming sector was left out of the visions of the governing soldiers whose interest was sharply focused on industrialization. The Sae Maul Campaign (New Village Movement) that started in 1969 in the rural sector and extended to the urban sector in 1975 changed this. It is a cultural and economic reform movement in the farming villages of the entire nation and is symbolized by the lead song "Jaal Sara Bose, meaning "Let's Live Beter-Off."[29]

Young workers idled by the winter cold after harvest volunteered to participate in village projects that straightened and paved the village roads to create better access to farms. Old grass roofs of farm residences were replaced by metal and slate roofs. Electricity and drinking water pipes were connected by these winter workers using the raw ma-

---

[29] I would have left out this section, for agriculture, in spite of its brilliant achievements, did not play the main role in the process of the Korean miracle. But the Sae Maul Movement continues today under the auspices of KOICA, the Korean International Cooperation Agency, planted the root of this movement in Africa, and South-East Asia as rural renewal programs and reports substantial success in turning the poor hopeless farmers to independent agri-business men.

terials and designs provided by the government budgets. Simple farming machines were created and supplied to all farms in generous installment financing, and they changed the farming methods completely. A new high-yield species of rice was developed by a scientist of the government's Agricultural Research Institute, and produced the world's highest yield per square meter of land. The stagnant farming sector of Korea became filled with hope and confidence that things could improve after all the long stagnation. Now Korean government has to set a budget every year for purchasing excess rice harvest every year to keep the domestic rice price high.

This nationwide campaign demonstrated how the temporal surplus of rural labor can successfully be combined with government-supplied construction materials such as cement, vinyl covers and steel bars for hot houses for winter farming. In Korea, most of the strawberry supply comes in January, not June, because winter strawberry is more expensive. Soon the urban manufacturing sector joined in this campaign with donations of materials to the farmers and this village renewal campaign became a nationwide movement. At 6:30 am every morning the entire nation woke up and gathered at the village central plaza to do national calisthenics following the same tune broadcast through loudspeaker. You don't need communist-style coercion when the entire nation is excited by the expectation of becoming better off, or even wealthy. In the late sixties and early seventies, Korea became a boiling pot.

After 50 years, this *New Village Campaign* has mostly disappeared in Korea as most members of the farming sector have gone to cities and overseas, or they have simply aged, but the campaign officials continue by spreading and proselytizing to many young men of African villages with the help of Korean volunteer workers and students similar to the American Peace Corp. Useless and unused lands are turned into rich farmlands growing expensive crops like rice, fresh vegetables, and animals in villages of Africa.

Thus the three necessary conditions for an economic take-off; peace, democracy, and a market economy are satisfied, and the sufficient condition of setting up a large middle class that plays the key role in the drama of economic growth and social changes is met. We even created a corporate sector by forcing reluctant entrepreneurs to join in the process of making a new history. These Jaebols with their GTC as their surveillance squad at the front and the government at the control tower, the team of Korea stood at the starting line. The savage war even prepared the collective mindset of the people, government, military, and corporations to join in this historical aviation. They all agreed that there was no alternative but to launch the economy. The aircraft left the ground.

An aircraft is safe while it is on the ground but is exposed to the dangers of crash once it takes off. The most important lesson from the Korean experience is that one should meticulously prepare to have sufficient energy for lifting and thrusting. Insufficient energy and power for the thrust will cause the aircraft to crash. In industrializing an economy, the power and thrust come from the international competitiveness of your new industries. You can subsidize your exporting corporations but only for a while. Like an eagle, the wings should gain muscles while flying. That is the ability to make continuous profit. After the take-off, the entire nation should focus on maintaining and raising the international competitiveness of its industries.

# Unique Trajectory

# VI. Road That Others Should Not Tread

## Heavy Mechanical, Petrochemical and Electronic (HMPE) Industries

The narration about Korea so far has been about a poor country struggling hard to take-off. The first five-year plan was the modest achievement of building a bridgehead for the creation of an industrial state. But the most significant trophy of the first five-year plan was the confidence it planted in the minds of people, engineers, scientist, the government, and the entrepreneurs. In a matter of ten years, the Korean business community learned how to organize corporations by drawing capital from stock buyers, create marketing networks by opening offices for sales and material-equipment acquisitions all over the world, and long-term financing and leasing of capital equipment.

Rapid growth in exports of light industrial products such as garments, textiles, and shoes facilitated the growth of corporations, and they started to plan the next level of growth from among the portfolio of major American, German, and Japanese companies. Electronics, overseas coal and iron ore mining, machine industries, shipbuilding, automobiles, petroleum and petrochemical industries, steel, airlines, cargo shipping, and construction, are some of the examples that corporations and government planners agreed on as their next targets. A substantial part of this book is devoted to the hardship Korea experienced in making these industries viable in a developing country. No poor country ever challenged this road of HMPE, for poor countries have no competitive advantage in them. Cheap wage is no help when one doesn't have an access to the advanced technology HMPE require. Many including some Korean intellectuals were certain that this Korean venture will fail.

Indeed, the outlook of these large-scale projects was dark. We did not have any advantage either in technology, the domestic market, parts and components supply, experience, or in transportation to the major markets of the world. But by now in the late 1960s Korean corporations were running offices for exports of products and imports of materials in altogether over one hundred countries. Through 10 years of experience, they created networks of international and Korean agents connecting all the major cities of the world including those in Africa. In the 60's the international scale of operation gave competitiveness to our light industries. But in the 70s, the required scale of operation grew by over 10-fold. The global network of operations and intelligence it produced was our advantage.

Both the market and the suppliers of HMPE industries are largely in rich advanced industrial countries and the poor countries are neither capable of supplying the products nor able to buy them on any meaningful scale. Korea wanted to enter into this industry but soon discovered that this industry is tightly protected by a gigantic exclusive invisible cartel of trust based on long successful experiences of reliability by the major western corporations. Unlike garments and shoes, purchasing HMPE goods requires a systematic test of the quality and durability as well as productivity, HMPE products are durable capital goods, and buying them is equivalent to investing in the future. The non-durable consumer goods market is very tolerant to newcomers, for the quality difference is minimal and even if one chooses the wrong brand, the impact of the error will last less than a month. But in HMPE, the impact of a bad decision lasts for years. There is virtually no room for newcomers. We needed a shock of some sort.

The shock actually came. The first oil shock, which raised the crude oil price from less than three dollars a barrel to over twelve dollars, came as a blessing for Korea. Suddenly all the major corporations started to be very cautious. High energy costs raised almost all the prices, and wages, entailing a serious downturn in business cycles. Hence the world entered into an unprecedented experience of depression with inflation; stagflation. Huge-scale infrastructure projects were mostly written off in the post-Vietnam USA and stagnant Europe.

Oil-rich Middle Eastern countries on the other hand opened their purses with their world-class engineering and construction projects. These new customers were far more open-minded compared to the conservative traditional clients of the rich first world. They did not have any love to the old colonial masters in Europe or the meddling American corporations. All Korea had to prove was that it could construct seaports, highways, airports, marine petroleum platforms, and tall buildings quickly, safely, and cheaply to win international biddings. The lack of experience and good references mattered far less. The invisible old exclusive cartel which dominated the HMPE industries was not as powerful as before.

There is one important episode that summarizes the situation well. One day president Park called Mr. Chung Ju Young of Hyundai to the Blue House and presented his problem. The president said that a few Mid-Eastern dollar-rich governments enquired at Korean embassies whether the Korean construction industry could join in the civil engineering projects in their desert lands. Korean civil engineering companies by now had some international recognition for their successful completion of the construction of the Seoul-Busan freeway, and the Vietnam expedition to assist the US armed forces in setting up their military bases and strategic infrastructure. The president immediately dispatched a team of Korean specialists and they reported that the desert countries were too hot in temperature and impractical to accommodate and control a large workforce.

Besides, the water supply is one critical bottleneck in carrying out any construction project but that is the hardest thing to get in the desert countries. Construction companies of rich countries would have hesitated to take up the project for these reasons.

That day Mr. Chung flew to Middle East and came back to report to the president in just five days. He reported that the desert countries are God-given opportunities for the construction industry. Rainy days are the worst enemy for construction works, and in these countries you can work for 365 days a year without the disturbance of rain. Sand is expensive raw material in construction works but sand is ubiquitous and free of charge there. When the air is hot during the day, the workers can sleep and when it becomes cool at night, they can work comfortably. As for water, I can load empty oil tankers with fresh water in smaller containers after they unloaded in Korean ports, and send them to the desert countries cheap.

Korean construction companies were able to put proposals together which under-priced traditional competitors, who demanded special compensation for the hard work environment. Normally our competitors offered very generous financial assistance to the project owners and Korea was easily dropped from the game. But the new Middle Eastern project owners were cash-rich and insensitive to financial assistance. Besides, Koreans had a decisive advantage; they promised a short-completion time.

Our strategy of a minimum delivery time at the lowest bidding price attracted the decision makers in the desert countries. We reinvented the work process and rescheduled the traditional process to improve speed and efficiency. Some of the steel structures to be installed at the Port of Juveil, Saudi Arabia, were manufactured and assembled in Korea to save time and cost, then brought to Saudi on an open barge over 7000 km by sea. Koreans behaved as if Neptune was on their side.

As discussed in more detail in the chapter dealing with the Jaebol issue, major Korean construction companies are members of a larger conglomerate group which owns independent companies specializing in backward linkage industries, such as intermediate material, mining and manufacturing components, and forward linkage industries such as international trading, building offices and apartments. They started to outsource the manufacturing process of their final-goods all over the world and called it OEM process. Australian iron ore turned into steel in Korea, and became the skin and engine of a car in Mexico to be sold in America in Hyundai brand. This multinational organization enabled the operation of multiple sites of construction simultaneously. Bulk-buying materials such as cements, steel bars, or by manufacturing them within the group, and easier transportation gave a distinct advantage in saving cost and time. With efficiency we compensated for our lack of experience.

## Blind Courage or Timely Wisdom

Some readers should now start to suspect the blind courage Korean corporate owners and government planners in starting projects that could have wrecked the entire ship. At the beginning of 70s Korea was already near the top of the list of global suppliers of goods in light industries. China was still sleeping and Japan was busy with HMPE industries. If Japan is doing well in HMPE industries, we should challenge this territory for *whatever the Japanese do, we can do better*, was the national psyche. Japan spent over a century to establish the world class industrial base. Koreans thought they should do the same in ten years.

This was not what was expected of the four dragons from the point of view of advanced industrial countries. Their role was to accept the outdated technology of mass-produced goods with huge market still alive strong in advanced countries.[30] The economic and industrial structures of NICs, namely newly industrializing countries, were expected to be complementary to European, American and Japanese industries by concentrating in industries less intensive in capital and technology. But Korea wanted to compete against the global leaders in industries where the technology was not mature, productivity was still rising, markets were still growing, and the high profit rate has still a long way to go. This was a sacrilege. If Koreans were wise enough at the beginning of the 1970s, we wouldn't have started the HMPE ventures. We didn't know it is called the value-chain optimization. We just wanted to beat

---

[30] We will discuss this phenomenon in next chapter. It is called international division of labor in production process in economics or value chain of supply in management.

the competition.

Korea started the adventure into the HMPE industries because they did not have the concept of global planning and optimizing global industrial networks. Because they did not have any friends in HMPE networks they neither had enough relevant intelligence nor any debt to insiders of the industries. As the Middle Eastern dollar owners opened their purses by inviting bids for major domestic projects, such as highways, bridges, new towns and harbors, Koreans simply joined the bidding parade and turned out to be the cheapest bidders. The mid-Eastern project owners didn't have any special love in the exclusive but invisible cartel of giant corporations of Europe and America. The Islam governments did not have any special connection or owe any favors to the major companies of the Christian world. They were always able to select any Euro-American companies to supervise and inspect the work in progress that was awarded to Koreans, and they did. That gave great educational opportunity to Koreans.

Once the bids were won, the projects progress became national championship games to Koreans where the entire country was drawn in for victory; namely to deliver the final outcome in time, and in internationally acceptable quality. That naturally destroyed the potential profits of Korean companies. Korean companies had to shorten the delivery time and save interest cost by early payments of bank loans, and that compensated for their loss of profit. This is one of the origins of the Korean Bali Bali culture. Koreans therefore changed the rules of game from maximizing profit to minimizing time of delivery and reducing costs. The global insiders of the cartels based on friendship and trust were able to do little to prevent this revolution. They had to follow or drop out. Korea started from a background of near impossibility and changed it to a possibility. The Korean HMPE strategy was one such paradoxical transformation that made impossibility into a possibility.

No narration of Korean development should miss this heroic story of Chairman Chung, Ju Young. Against everybody's expectation, he succeeded in getting a contract for building the two world's largest oil tankers with only a picture of a Korean fishing village where he planned to build a dockyard to build ships. He didn't have any experience in shipbuilding, and he didn't have any technology for it.

All he had was his dream and confidence that shipbuilding was similar to erecting buildings for which he had enough experience. He thought the basic design would be given by the ship-owners and all he had to do was to follow the instructions given by the experienced western planners, designers, and supervisors he employed.

He started by seeking loans for building the dock, and no banks took him seriously. After a series of many failed meetings he finally went to London where he met an officer of Barkley's Bank. This British gentleman was kind enough to explain to Mr. Chung the proper process for borrowing money for shipbuilding, and told Mr. Chung the preconditions for getting a loan was to get a contract for shipbuilding from commercial fleet owners. Mr. Chung made an appointment with the owner of Livanos Group and he went to the meeting alone at his Swiss chalet. When he came out from the Livanos residence at about 2.00 am next morning, Mr. Chung had in his hand a contract for building two oil tankers of 220,000 metric tons each. The world never saw such big vessels before. Chances are that Mr. Livanov protected himself by insuring for the failure of delivery but this stubborn young Korean businesman actually delivered the miracle in time.

This adventure into the HMPE territory by Korean companies carries a very important implication to all the developing counties of the world and in setting the future development trajectory for Korea. Without world class corporations in the HMPE industries, no country can join the highest income group in the world. With only light industrial exports such as textiles and shoes, one cannot escape the middle income trap. The decision to enter into HMPE requires a series of very hard decisions. For instance in 1966, when Korea decided to establish an integrated steel mill in Pohang, the World Bank specialists refused to lend money. The best they could do was *not to object* to the POSCO project that used the reparation money from Japan. Korea did not have any comparative advantage in the steel industry, and bank money lent to other steel mills construction projects in developing countries ended with massive losses, and many of them at least had iron ore mines. But Korea had neither an iron ore mine, nor the technology for integrated steel mill. Today POSCO is rated as the most profitable steel company in the world and has subsidiaries in power generation, general trading company, construction, and nickel refining. Postech, a globally renowned engineering university owns the controlling share of this group, where I had the honor of serving as a member of the board.

In the early 70s, no Koreans cared about joining the highest-income group in the world, for it was a concept far beyond reality. But we just had to enter into the tough world of HMPE industries because there were highly profitable opportunities far beyond the light industrial markets, and the Japanese were very successful in HMPE industries. That was reason enough for the Korean private sector planners. But in the minds of public policymakers, American withdrawal from Vietnam posted a new parameter in the international relationships—nobody will protect Korean democracy if a war turns messy and long. The US withdrawal from Vietnam was a clear signal that we should develop our own independent deterrence. For self-defense Korea needed a powerful weapons industry and that comes only from the strong and healthy HMPE industries. Taiwan assumed their 'Semiconductor Shield' will protect them from the invasion of China, and neglected other HMPE industries. Today nobody, including the Taiwanese, believes that they can defend Taiwan by themsleves.

HMPE ventures naturally led to massive borrowing, and when recessions hit, HMPE investments became non-performing quicker than small and light industries. When the 1997 economic crisis came, most of the adjustments of excess investment took place in the HMPE industries. In an ironic way, the adventure into HMPE became the reason for both the crisis due to over borrowing, as well as the ultimate tool that brought Korea world class prosperity. And Korea had the luck and wisdom as well as the courage that other dragons lacked.

## Seed for New Industrial Ambition

Corporations of the industrialized economies have now begun to organize the entire world in their scheme of a multinational allocation of segments of production process. This decision is based on assessments of the competitive advantages of each country considering the cost of production that includes labor, capital, and technology along with socio-political attitudes to foreign investment according to

Professor Michael Porter of Harvard Business School. We now call that a value chain system.

To the eyes of industrial economists, the labor force can be trained either by the government or companies who need the manpower with some government assistance. Entrepreneurs come from anywhere, both domestic and international, so long as there is a good profit-making chance. Usually, the government raises the success probability to over 90% by adding various sweeteners to attract foreign investors. Low wages attract the attention of planners of the rich corporation, but actual investment decision is made after long negotiations between the foreign companies and the hosting government. Wage levels in Slovakia are more than twice that of Myanmar but Hyundai's automobile assembly plant is located in Slovakia to serve the markets of Western Europe. Production cost is just one consideration among so many factors.

From the office of the hub company in New York, Chicago, Frankfurt, and Tokyo access to the final market was a far more important consideration than the agility and innovativeness of the workers and local businessmen of the host country. Since Singapore and Hong Kong cannot be turned into a manufacturing centers, they remained as transshipment ports and bunkering ports with fresh supplies. That made Mexico, Brazil, Argentine, Spain, Ireland, the Balkan countries, Turkey, Korea, and Taiwan good candidates for industrial migration. Without China on the scene in the early 1980s, the world was divided nicely into industry-emigrating countries and countries that hosted immigrating companies. Number of successful hosting countries remained a little over ten for a decade.[31]

One important dynamic consideration in building a global supply chain is the issue of transporting *parts and components*. In the initial stages, hub companies send fully assembled final products and decomposed them into about five parts before shipping, letting the host company reassemble the products and enjoy lower tariffs. This practice was called the semi-knockdown method (SKD), which preceded the complete knock-down (CKD), and both are

---

[31] Economists were quick to point out the lack of absorptive capacity, blaming the shortage of trained manpower and lack of entrepreneurs who should organize the labor. Nobel laureate Prof. Robert Lucas addressed this issue in his published lecture on the Korean Miracle in which he described the difference in the growth performance of Korea and the Philippines as coming from different learning curves. We will address this later. The high-growth performance of the Four Asian Dragons in the 1980s attracted all sorts of economic and social explanations in the name of absorptive capacity. They even invoked the traditional religion of the Asian Dragons, Confucianism.

called OEM, a strange name for an outsourced assembly process. Since there are many alternative candidates competing to host the new industry, poor governments not only allowed this technical illegality but also added sumptuous monetary assistance through various tax exemptions and cash payments.

As time passed, some countries such as Brazil, Spain, Taiwan, and Korea started to domestically produce several important components, and government policies required that these new components be used by the hosting local companies. Needless to say, the locally produced components were cheaper than those produced in hub countries, and this strengthened the competitiveness of their joint products. It is only natural for the hub company to prevent the host company from exporting its product to the international markets and competing against the hub company's product. But such prevention did not last long for the host company's technology improved continuously, and the monetary loss from preventing imports of low-cost products became too high.[32] The whole game started with trans-

---

[32] FT-50 is a jet-fighter pilot training aircraft jointly designed by Lockheed-Martin and KAI, Korean Aerospace Industries, and exclusively produced by KAI. It was banned to supply to the US air force by Lockheed-Martin until their own version of the refurbished F16

porting parts and components to NICs to assemble the final products to be imported to the hub country. Like the fool moon, the competitiveness of rich countries shrinks too, but the rich companies survive by importing the final products made in NICs.

It took another 30 years for the host companies in Korea to defeat the hub companies of rich industrial countries in this game. Occasionally the products of challengers demonstrated better performance, quality, and durability, which is what happened with semiconductor chips made in Taiwan and Korea. We will discuss this in more detail in chapters on technology and Jaebol. At this stage in the 1990s and early 2000, Korea was alone in challenging the best and strongest in the world. The other three NICs took the safer road of harmonious coexistence with hub companies, but Korea couldn't tolerate the selfish and predatory business strategies of the Japanese semiconductor industry and almost by instinct, Samsung rammed through Sharp, Hitachi, and Toshiba with price competitiveness based on new and superior technology. Korea was the first country that understood that to remain viable in high-tech HMPE

---

turned out a marketing failure for the expensive price tag. This market is wide open now.

industries, one should not enter the low end of the market, but challenge the top of the market where there are far fewer competitors and a blue ocean is waiting for you.


## The Case of Semiconductor

Samsung made two major decisions that laid the lasting foundation of the Samsung semiconductor business. In 1983 when Samsung was planning to enter into this totally unknown industry, every afternoon on the 28th floor of the Samsung headquarters building, Mr. Byung Chul Lee held a meeting with a dozen selected Korean brains which included four professional semiconductor specialists just returned from Silicon Valley, California. Rest of us had great difficulty in understanding what the specialists were talking about. We repeated meetings for nearly half a year covering the same ground over and over again, namely on the merits and risks of mass-producing memory chips, which is called the commodity ICs, against the safer semiconductors for consumer electronics, which is far easier with very low risk. Mr. Lee finally decided to challenge the high risk-high return memory chips. If we selected the low-technology consumer electronics ICs then, Samsung and Korea must be about 15 years behind Taiwan by now, a tiny bit ahead of China. He bet on the potentially superior Korean production technology that required a large scale of production. In hindsight, it was a brilliant decision that made Korea a supplier of 75% in the global memory chip market.

At around this time, the US and Japanese governments were negotiating on the VAR, a voluntary restraint agreement, whereby the US wanted the Japanese to restrain from cutting the semiconductor prices and Japan wanted to cut the price freely to monopolize the market. IBM, HP, Texas Instrument etc. , the semiconductor users supported the lower price, and Intel, Micron, and Motorola, the US IC makers were on the side supporting higher prices. Samsung's production cost of memory chips was at the breakeven point. Mr. Lee bet on the US semiconductor makers instead of the IC users such as IBM. He knew that President Reagan will support the weak but futuristic IC industry instead of the powerful computer makers. In 1986 he directed to double the semiconductor production capacity to prepare for the market that will bring in huge profit.

Within the same year, Samsung successfully designed the *One mega Dynamic Random Access Memory Chip* (DRAM) for the first time in the world. With the arrival of personal computers and Microsoft's operational system, the world started to understand the explosive use of semiconductors already in the 80s, and the arrival of the the internet with World Wide Web in early 90s reinforced this expectation. Samsung had to invest massively when the investment cost is the lowest, namely in downturn of the cycle. But our rivals in Japan thought the downturn is a bad time to invest. And when the boom in demand came back, as Mr. Moor of Intel predicted, we won huge profits naturally in every 18 months. Our adversaries call that a chicken game because of the nerve it requires but our nerve came from our trust in the Korean engineers and workers in our clean fab rooms.

Five years after Samsung began the semiconductor adventure, he died of recurred cancer. Nobody knows whether he believed that Korea will become the 8th richest country in the world and his semiconductor investment made the critical breakthrough leading Korea into the rich man's land.[33] There was an unwritten social convention in Korea

---

[33] He expressed his extraordinary conviction that the superior ability of the Korean

those days that in order to merely survive, we have to go all the way up to challenge the best and strongest corporations in the world. The seed of industrial ambition was cast almost by instincts.

## Dismantling an Authoritarian Governance

Korea's venture into the HMPE industries owes greatly to the authoritarian military government because a democratically elected government with a critical opposition party looking over the shoulder cannot sustain this unpopular campaign while repeating missteps and crises. Like the take-off at the beginning, Korea owes significantly to the guts and drives of insensitive soldiers who acted only according to their conviction and patriotism.

Another major stumbling block on the way to the mature HMPE industries was bad timing. Korea had barely ten years of experience at the end of the 70s in the international construction, shipbuilding, cars, and petrochemical

workforces and scientists will prevail over the world one day. I don't know the basis of his faith as yet. We certainly did not have much evidence for this conviction especially 40 years ago.

industries. The second world oil crisis in which oil prices increased from 12-15 dollars to 40-45 dollars overnight, came with another crisis: the assassination of President Park who barely a half a year earlier has announced the ending of government-led five-year plans, and replaced them by *indicative plans* that put private corporations first with the government following behind. Most Koreans didn't understand the ramification of this change. The second Korean military coup followed, and the US president-elect tried to withdraw US ground forces from Korea. The bloody suppression of street demonstrators in the city of Gwangju by the new military junta shocked the world. Korea was in a mess and the inevitable policy to create a *Korean defense industry* was formally adopted. This policy required a stronger government, but it is taken by a government that just gave up government-led planning.

Post-Soviet Russia under President Boris Yeltzin is a good example of how to mess up freedom and democracy and send the nation into a chaos during times of explosive changes, but that is beyond the subject of this book. However, it must be pointed out that the orderly change of China into a market economy in the early 1990s depended on the carefully designed transition policies that emulated the so-called Park, Chung Hee Model of South Korea. The point is when an *ancient regime* is dismantled; every society needs some form of antidote that prepares people to know how to honor the limit of individual freedom in this new free society. Unfortunately, the virus of communism is far too strong even in 2022 and killed all the vibrant cells of freedom in China.[34] The so called Park, Chung Hee Model has two parts; authoritarian strong government for takeoff and dismantling the authoritarian ruling and introducing free economy and polity. The latter is harder than the former.

## Spit on My Tomb

For Korea, the universal mandatory education system (1948) and the great land reform (1949) were two basic groundwork of long-term structural impact. The war(1950) and the flood of western culture provided the correct men-

---

[34] I must confess that in early 1990's, many Korean economists, including this writer, corporate managers, and engineers were repeatedly invited to China to lecture and debrief the *strong government model* of early Korean development stage. It still turns my face red in shame whenever I think about the conceited attitudes we then had shown to Chinese policy-maker hosts. Honestly China looked so weak and retarded after Tien An Men Squre. Little we knew then that they were merely pretending modesty.

tal shock to the mind of the community with the need for the honest pursuit of material well-being with no shame. Investment in the import substitution projects that replaced large-scale imports with domestic production gave the answer to the question of *where to start*. Recruiting the local merchants and forcing them to become modern entrepreneurs was the answer to the question of who will lead. The underlying principle in designing investment projects was to aim at the export markets and projects were, without exception, *scaled up until the cost of production declined to the internationally competitive price*. And the government took the responsibility of providing necessary financing and technology.

One big fault in this model of igniting the engine of industrial development is that the companies almost always failed to reduce their production costs to the internationally competitive level and made huge losses. Korea's answer to this problem was to make the projects and the companies profitable at any cost. All the projects included in the plan demanded huge imports of capital equipment, critical parts and components, and intermediate materials and energy. As the foreign exchange was in tight supply, these critical goods are always in short supply carrying huge margins in the domestic markets over the international import prices. Giving additional tariff-free quota for imports of these critical goods, which we called the license for smuggling, gave enough compensation to the losses the companies made. This is equivalent to subsidizing the rich importing country consumers of our finished goods using our scarce foreign exchanges and cheap wages in return for building the new Korean Industries.

The two-way flow of imports of critical goods and exports of our finished goods gave several important roles for the General Trading Companies. Korean industries, small or large, instantly gained access to global networks of trading services at an insignificant cost. All the exports were rewarded with sumptuous extra benefits to keep the exporting companies alive. But this extraordinary process of creating modern international corporations with global network and massive subsidies for exports entailed a strong criticism from the people, media, and academics. It was a combination of policies deliberately aiming to make the rich richer. Not only it was not fair, but it also was a tightrope walking over the borderline of illegality. In other words, this set of policies would have been impossible under a properly functioning democratic government. Economists nicely call this the *need for a strong government* at the start of development. General Park, Chung Hee, the head of the military junta that started the five-year economic plans was convinced that he was doing the right thing for the modernization of Korea and somebody has to do the dirty role. He knew how history will describe him years later. He actually arrested 30 merchants at the beginning of his coup for 'profiteering' and nobody could claim that he sided with the rich. He remained frugal and clean from corruption until his death, and fully aware of the historical role he was playing. He declared 'Spit on my tomb.'

However, he was aware of the damaging effect of a prolonged ruling by a strong government and abolished the government-led economic plans when the 3rd five-year plan finished. The plan afterward was the mere enunciation of only the desired goals of growth in each sector and the government stopped interfering with the private decisions of investment, except for the defense industry that started after the announcement of the Nixon Doctrine in early 1970. But he was assassinated before this change was actually implemented. One Stanford economics Ph.D. named Kim, Jae Ik continued this economic liberalization as the head of the Economic Committee of the Council of National Security, the transitory legislature plus administration set up by the new military junta until he also was assassinated by the North Korean bomb planted at the Burmese national cemetery. The end of strong governing is not peaceful and the transition cannot be seamless.

The name Arthur Lewis, Nobel laureate of Economics, is frequently borrowed to designate this turning point of political liberalization of developing countries[35] by commentators. The popular theory was that when the GNP per capita reached USD 5,000 in Korea or Spain, the private corporate sector's ability to predict the future, and plan for investment surpasses that of bureaucrats in terms of the quality of plans, and ability to carry them out. That turning point roughly coincided with the death of President Park. For China, we expected the per capita income of US 10,000 dollars would mark the turning point, but it did not happen. China is turning into an Orwellian Big-Brother so-

---

[35] His theory aims to determine the starting point of the balanced growth strategy for a wide range of industries and has little to do with predicting the dates when authoritarian military governments fall. But it gives a convenient concept for reference.

ciety and proved either the theory is wrong or the statistics of China is false, or both.

Liberal democracy with a freedom of expression and private property is what we have fought for at the expense of over a million lives. At the beginning of the take-off a strong government under a group of soldiers was tolerated as a lesser evil and inconvenience to fend off the permanent dictatorship by communists, and to free the society from traditional stagnation. But the hangover of strong governing demanded blood. We shed our share it. A society reaches a point in history, where it should make a courageous and wise decision to dismantle the overly concentrated power of government.

Deng, Shao Ping, for instance, read the deployment of history correctly and started to turn the wheel of China toward a market economy full of vitality and creativity. But when he came to the historical moment at the Tien An Men Square confrontation, he made a tragic mistake for which Chinese people is still paying the price. He believed that a market economy can continue and grow while maintaining communist dictatorship. Xi, Jin Ping is proving that there is no such thing as the *state capitalism* and that pseudo market economy under a communist dictatorship inevitably fails.

## Sad Experience of Defense Industry

With the prolonged war in Ukraine, some pariah-capitalist politicians in Washington began to cry for 'not a single penny more to Ukraine.' US weapons producers already confess that there is no more arms-manufacturing capability in the US to help others. By a strange fluke of history, Korea became the one and only potential arms exporter who can deliver necessary arms in time to defend the NATO members of Eastern Europe. To know how it happened, we should read to the end of this book, but I like to make it sure that Korea did not want or plan to be a global arms supplier. But the second push for Korea's HMPE industry came in the form of early warning for investment in the weapons industry to create an independent deterrence capability.

The totally unexpected birth of the oil cartel and oil price shocks gave Korean companies a new push to soft-land in the HMPE industries during the 70s. Post-Vietnam US politics gave new life to the Korean HMPE venture. The long-espoused *Domino Effect in Indo-China* after the fall of Saigon didn't happen after all. But the US role as the guarantor of peace and independence for Asian democracies was seriously damaged. The prevailing common sense was that the fall of South Korea by communist invasion would automatically entail the fall of Japan. But the fall of Saigon without the domino effect suddenly made the withdrawal of US ground forces from the Korean Peninsula a highly likely option. If Thailand did not fall after Saigon, why should Tokyo fall after the fall of Seoul?

The election of Jimmy Carter to the US presidency with his promise to withdraw GIs from Korea was permanently engraved in the minds of Koreans, along with new facts that a change in the US president or his judgment over the North East Asian security dynamics can easily change the status of US ground troops. Thus, there is nothing permanent in the US-Korea Joint Security Treaty. It is only natural that US domestic politics supersedes its international relationship.

A corollary follows: (1) Build your own independent and viable defense system, (2) Take advantage of the active alliance with the United States of America, but never believe that it is sufficient and durable, (3) Break the unwise dogma that the USA is the only viable alliance. Today's enemy can turn into a friend. Never use ideology as a criterion for making friends. Mr. Biden's actions in Afghanistan withdrawal and the new friendly gestures made by Mr. Putin of Russia to the Korean government reinforced this position.[36]

Although Carter failed in his planned withdrawal, the Korean government became obsessed with creating new viable defense industries in Korea. Shipbuilders were forced to build battleships and submarines, and railcar makers and automobile manufacturers were forced to build tanks and armored vehicles. Machine-making industries were turned into makers of artillery and rifles. The aircraft maintenance industry was turned into jet fighter makers. With the collateral market of government contracts with fixed margin

---

[36] It is reported that Mr. Putin wishes to permanently lend the Kamchatka Peninsula at the tip of the Siberian east coast to South Korea, and his delegates are negotiating the terms and conditions of the joint development project of Sakhalin Island with representatives of the South Korean government.

rates guaranteed, the companies shouldn't have lost money, but nearly all of them did.

The quality of weapons was poor and the weapons were unusable, and the development and inflow of foreign technology were slow. Much of the technology that Korean companies needed was simply not for sale for national security reasons. The world was inundated by the wave of the second oil crisis. President Park was assassinated in 1979, and the Korean polity fell into chaos. For the first time since it took off in 1962, Korea reported a minus 4.1% growth rate of the real GDP, and the wholesale price index rose as high as 42 % a year.

This coerced and compulsive jump into the defense industry left a legacy of massive overinvestment, and the hangover of this excess capacity remained as the cause of financial burdens of all weapon makers, until the Korean economic crisis in 1997 forced them into self-liquidations or forced buying out by bigger Korean weapon makers.[37]

---

[37] The scale and depth of this nationwide economic adjustment is reported in detail in the book, "Balancing between Panic and Mania – Asian Economic Crisis", 1999 in English by this author. It is safe to say that after the extensive liquidations and buying outs nearly all those weapon makers that belonged to a Jaebol groups survived and smaller companies disappeared.

At the beginning of the defense industry, most companies started from assembling imported components and parts. Unlike the export-oriented engineering, construction, and shipbuilding industries of the 70s, the defense industry of Korea that started at the end of the 70s aimed at the domestic government market, with near zero exports. That created a critical burden for the trade account balance and Korea fell deeply in structural balance-of-payment deficits that lasted until the crisis of 1997.

# VII. Unique Trajectory of the Lonely Dragon

## Industrial Migration and Wages

Japan started the game of lengthening the life cycles of mature products by manufacturing with cheap wages. Mature products are outdated consumer products that originally were made and sold in the US and European markets for decades. American and European companies invented the products long ago and developed huge markets in their own countries too good to ignore. As the number of suppliers grew, the market price inevitably went down to shrink the bottom lines of producers to unbearable levels, and made the continuation of domestic production impractical. They had to look toward international opportunities and invented two new concepts. One was the birth of the Multinational Corporations in the 1950s, I believe, and the second was the mass migration of industrial capital and facilities to where the production cost was lower. To understand the Korean miracle, one needs to understand the migration of industries for Korea started soaking up these industries possessing international mobility very actively.

The once unique monopoly technology became widely available by separating the product technology from the production technology. Major American corporations started to go rapidly multinational and drove stagnant Europeans to panic. They blamed themselves for some sort of congenital Euro-pessimism. Fifteen years after GIs went back home at the end of WWII, the Yankees came back with their production plants. And they called it the birth of *Multinational Corporation*. At the beginning, in the early 1960s, only labor-intensive segments of the production process were shifted to Japan or Germany by American corporations, but soon the local companies started to take up the same strategy as German and Japanese wages rose. To American companies, it was a simple change of the assembling location of outdated products to the vicinity of European and Japanese markets. To economists it was a great international division of labor of mature-product manufacturing, giving industrial capital the mobility to move around. To the Japanese and European companies, it was a great chance to beat the American companies in production cost reduction, quality improvement and marketing both in domestic and in American markets. The neat comparative advantage map became all messed up.

Once this process of industrial migration began, humans discovered an important new tool for fighting against poverty around the globe simultaneously. Corporations of the first-generation industrial migration from the USA, Europe and Japan, and companies of second generation migrants from Korea, Taiwan, and Spain jointly perfected this art of creating multi-regional value chains of supply by segmenting the production processes. In the 80s the segmentation was mainly between capital and the technology-intensive production process against the labor-intensive production processes. Pursuing cheaper-wage countries was the principal motivation for migration, and it is still true. But in the 21st century the global optimization of the value chains of supply/production has become highly sophisticated.

For instance, in the case of semiconductor production, the chain is divided into (1) designing the product, mainly by US, Korean and British companies, both memories and systems on chips, (2) outsourcing the development of critical components and parts to domestic and international suppliers thus creating a multinational network of exclusive supplier networks (mainly by US, Japan, Korea, Netherland and Germany), (3) applying the same strategy to invent and supply higher versions of entirely new materials and creating dedicated new equipment frequently requiring very high technology (Netherland, Sweden, Korean, US), (4) fabricating the treated silicon wafers and manufacturing integrated circuits, (mainly by Taiwan, USA, Korea) and (5) special packaging to make the product conveniently usable by final consumers.

But for the simple mature products such as color TVs of the 1980s, the production process was divided into (1) designing a color TV (Japan, Korea, USA, France, and Germany). (2) Making parts such as producing the printed circuit board, cathode-ray tubes, and speakers (Taiwan, Malaysia, Korea, Japan) and (3) Assembling the final products and making plastic cases domestically. (Philippines, Malaysia, Indonesia). Segmentation of supply activities was differentiated over countries not as much by capital intensiveness but mainly by the availability of technology. Readers will find eventually that capital became mobile, but technology is not. Over time as the final products become more sophisticated, the supply chain becomes technologically more complicated.

## Four Asian Dragons and China

What the world saw at the beginning of the 1980s, namely the rise of the four dragons of East Asia, was the primitive early version of the international division of labor, so simple that economists called that the goose flying pattern. It was not wrong, but there is something seriously hollow in their observation. Like a powerful whirlpool, all the poor countries with people who had a decent level of education are drawn into this new system of industrial manufacturing mobility. The impact of this giant whirlpool that crashed the thousand-year-old poverty is magnificent, to say the least. Never had humans seen a billion people join in the revolution of employment opportunity, and lifestyle through urbanization in this magnitude. China and India are prime examples. Korea became one of the richest countries in the world through this process of industrial mobility.

More than three- quarters of the countries on earth are underdeveloped and are mostly not developing. This model of industrial migration is spreading this wealth-creating systems and devices all around the world. This is the answer to the destructive communist model of forced redistribution of a fixed pie making everybody equally poor. This model of industrial migration is not a theory but a reality. It is the historic Manifesto of Anti-Communism. Some fail in hosting and nurturing a lasting industrial sector, but some succeed in continuing economic growth by actively sending out old industries and hosting new industries. Some even succeed in turning itself into a rich country in a global standard.

Economics does not deserve the respect it receives if people don't expect that this science can bring in the Wealth for a Nation, namely by driving away the poverty. The corporate sector presents an effective model for building the wealth of nations and crushing the chronic sickness of poverty. Industrial migration is eradicating poverty all around the world. But the sophisticated professional academics and practitioners of economics seem unimpressed by this whirlpool of industrial mobility and remain so detached. Higher national wealth is the reflection of the greater wealth-creating capability that comes from higher investments. Higher investment takes place only when the corporate sector generates good profits. But in microeconomics, a good profit is taken as evidence that the supply price is too high and there is not enough competition in the market to push it down.

As the wages of the leading goose rose, its industries migrated to other rising dragons, and as the wages of the dragons rose, industries further migrated to other parts of the Western Pacific. ASEAN countries enthusiastically joined in this game toward the end of the 1980s. But when China, after the Tien An Men Massacre, managed to join the WTO in the early 90s, it practically hijacked almost all of the industrial migration. This preempted ASEAN opportunities of hosting new industries. The ex-factory price of a video recorder from the Samsung Suwon Plant ranged from around US$150 to 180, the same from Samsung's Malaysian plant was US$120 to 140, and the Chinese exported the same product at US$50 FOB. Korea had to close down all the video plants in the world to set up plants in China.

Wages in the consumer electronic industry constitute less than 10% of the total cost. Wage differences between Malaysia and China cannot explain the export-price difference of 250%. Only massive government subsidy can.

The rapid accumulation of dollar reserves by the Chinese Central Bank once reached 4.5 trillion dollars due to their excessive trade surplus. But most academic economists compare the differences in price rises between China and the rest of the world and concluded that the insignificant difference in the inflation rates between China and its trading partners provided evidence that China's exchange ratio was not undervalued. The fact is that from the starting point of early the 1980s, when China started to join the global market as an exporter of light industrial goods, the yuan was seriously and arbitrarily undervalued, and subsequent observations were just evidence that the yuan was *not further de-valued* compared to the initial undervaluation. But to the eyes of the public, the view of the academic economists was unbiased, and industrial economists like this author were biased in favor of competitors against China.

However, twenty-five years later China's wages rose

naturally[38] and the direction of industrial migration shifted to South East Asia. ASEAN members belatedly started to join the global supply chain of the industrial division of labor. This 20[th-] century version of division of the labor in the production process leads the managers of *production technology research centers*[39] (not Product Research Centers) to draw production- cost map of the world. They allocate subsets of the production processes to each country, the least-cost segment of the supply chain most suitable to that country. Cheaper wages of South East Asia beat China now in attracting labor-intensive segments of production and most of the technology-intensive segments either remained at home bases or were sent to countries neighboring the final markets where the economic environments were similar to the final markets. Hungary and Slovakia are good examples.

## Thorn Bush for Direct Investment

A country which is popular for foreign direct investment

---

[38] China's minimum wage announced by the Beijing government in 2021 is almost half of the Korean minimum wage level.

[39] This concept will be discussed in detail later at the chapter of Technology Nationalism.

is popular for loans as well. There are three main channels that foreign capital flows in – direct investment, portfolio investment, and bank loans. A poor developing country's access to foreign investment is selling government-issued bonds. There are more than 200 countries in the world and foreign investors and lenders should be meticulous in selecting one candidate each time for investment or lending to the poor government. Naturally this selection process is far more stringent than the selection process of Miss Universe. Valuable seeds should not be planted under a thorn bush.

Foreign Direct Investment (FDI) entails very little immediate financial burden to the local economy for there is no annual interest payment. Loans should be paid back but the FDI requires dividends only when sufficient profit is generated by the investment. FDI comes with technology assistance from the investing company engineers whose know-how, frequently unwritten, is quite valuable and helpful in reaching the optimum level of operation of machines and equipment in the shortest time period. FDI comes with the managerial experience of the well-seasoned executives and staffs who help to assure profits, not to speak of the employment generation and income from taxes.

But FDI has several shortcomings including unfair marketing territory disputes. From the point of view of the investing company, FDI should not be permitted to become a tool for creating a competitor. The host company is strictly prohibited from exporting to countries where the investor company is exporting. But the investor usually competes in the local markets where their investment is made. The real conflict arises when dividends are determined. The investor wants maximum dividends for it does not want to help the local partner grow and become an international competitor. This is directly against the goal of the local host and the country that needs to grow.

It is highly unlikely that a country is favored for direct investment but unpopular for receiving loans. The country may be chosen for direct capital investment in a joint venture together with a local partner investor, or the foreign investor may have 100% ownership, either way liquidity lending follows for operational purposes or organizing supplier networks of local component manufacturers. If the country is unsuitable for direct investment because there is a threat of terror or a war with a neighbor, it will be unsuitable for lending as well. Korea again proved to be an exception to this common sense. Permit me to quote a table from my book. Korea is one of the toughest places in the world to invest and make profits for foreign investors. This table explains that Korea stands out as a heavy borrower with low popularity. Most of the statements in this book are well-known and demand no particular evidence, but the statements from now are so peculiar to Korea that I felt that some sort of statistical evidence is necessary.

### Foreign Debt as Share of GDP (1997)

| | Total Foreign Debt (USD bill.) | GDP (USD bill.) | Foreign Debt/GDP (%) |
|---|---|---|---|
| Korea | 71.6 | 490.1 | 14.6 |
| Malaysia | 34.4 | 87.8 | 39.1 |
| Thailand | 56.8 | 182.7 | 31.1 |
| Indonesia | 107.8 | 225.8 | 47.7 |
| Philippines | 39.4 | 83.5 | 47.2 |

Source; Balancing between Panic and Mania—The East Asian Economic Crisis and Challenges to Internal Financing, Ungsuh Kenneth Park, Samsung Economic Research Institute Press. 2000

From the penthouse offices in New York and Chicago Korea is so far away and insignificant compared to Japan and China. The population is less than half that of Japan, technology is far behind and there are many other places that are far safer than Korea. In the early part of its rapid growth, the 60s and 70s, both foreign direct investment and loans from foreign private banks remained low. But international borrowing through a public channel, the Korea Development Bank, was very active reaching 71.6 billion US dollars by 1997. But as the table shows, the Korean economy, which was 5 times as large as Philippines and Malaysia, or at least twice as large as Indonesia, the inflow of foreign capital was lower than Indonesia, and not much above the other ASEAN countries.

As if it was not miserable enough, the Korean foreign direct investment data shows a sadder story. The foreign capital inflow to Korea was merely 14.5 % of the GDP but Korea's annual FDI compared to GDP remained below 1% consistently.[40] Measured in a ratio of FDI as percent of GDP Korea was about as attractive as China in 1984, that was when the communist China was just about beginning to open its door and was busy fighting with Vietnam. See first table in footnote. In terms of FDI/GDP Korea was never as popular as China except the corona days. Hong Kong

---

[40] The above table of FDI/GDP is derived by dividing the data of FDI to East Asia (upper table of this foot note) by GDP of East Asia of this footnote (lower table).

belonged to a different club altogether.

## FDI/GDP (%)

| | 1984 | 1987 | 1997 | 2008 | 2019 |
|---|---|---|---|---|---|
| China | 0.45 | 0.7 | 4.71 | 2.36 | 0.1 |
| Hong Kong | 3.8 | 12.35 | 6.41 | 26.59 | 18.69 |
| Korea | 0.23 | 0.56 | 0.65 | 0.21 | 0.64 |

## FDI to East Asia ($Mill)

| | 1984 | 1987 | 1997 | 2008 | 2019 |
|---|---|---|---|---|---|
| China | 1,419 | 2,314 | 45,257 | 108,312 | 141,225 |
| Hong Kong | 1,288 | 6,250 | 11,368 | 58,315 | 68,379 |
| Korea | 223 | 839 | 3,301 | 11,188 | 10,566 |

## GDP of East Asia ($Mill)

| | | | | | |
|---|---|---|---|---|---|
| China | 313,723 | 327,090 | 961,601 | 4,554,337 | 14,342,934 |
| Hong Kong | 33,511 | 50,623 | 177,353 | 217,279 | 365,711 |
| Korea | 97,511 | 147,969 | 509,755 | 1,047,339 | 1,646,539 |

(This is UNCTAD data and the GDP data above is IMF data)
Source; UNCTAD-Stat. Balance of Payment- FDI, and GDP

Furthermore, there is a clear bias toward lending over investing in Korea. Out of 71 billion dollars of foreign capital that came to Korea in 1997, only 3.3 billion dollars were in the form of FDI.[41] Even after 68 years of rapid growth, only a few think Korea is a place to invest and make profits. It is too far away, too cold, too dangerous, and different.

This bias to loan was not Korea's choice. Loan through a public bank owned by the Korean government was the only window foreigners wanted to use. Koreans didn't have a choice. In the long run, however, this bias toward loans proved to be an advantage in terms of corporate management. Korean corporations were able to decide autonomously where and when to invest, and what products to invest in without interference from the headquarters in New York or Tokyo, whose tendency was to ban their subsidiaries from competing against the mother companies. FDI always comes with a specific purpose even if the host country is a very attractive destination. The purpose is to produce export goods near or inside huge markets. However, investors strictly forbid the subsidiary in a developing country from competing against the home office. Subsidiaries are strictly forbidden from exporting the same products to countries where the home office exports. But usually, the

---

[41] According to the UNCTAD report out of 50 years between 1970 to 2019, FDI reached Korean shore surpassed 1% of GDP of Korea in just five years, 1974, 2001, 2004, 2005,and 2018.

home office exports the same products to the subsidiary's domestic market separately.

The worse intervention by the home office is the prohibition of technological independence of the subsidiary by forcing the subsidiary to follow a non-expiring technological dependence agreement even if the subsidiary is only partially owned by the home office. As we will see below, the key to Korea's rise to the position of global industrial power was its technological nationalism. By relying on borrowed capital, Korean corporations managed to keep their autonomy in deciding what industry to step into or what technology to develop or buy. Every bad thing seems matched by a good thing like the Korean national flag. Some seeds thrown under the thorn bush grow stronger than those grown in hot houses.

## Economic Development by Borrowing

Korea was not an outstanding goose in the squadron called flying geese, the name given in economic textbooks. Two English-speaking city-states, Hong Kong and Singapore were exposed to European and American culture, and to international trading for over 150 years. Their commerce and law were comfortable to the western investors. They achieved high-income status without serious industrialization by taking advantage of the strategic location in international trading. Taiwan was almost 15 years ahead of Korea with its carefully-made plans for and its execution of industrialization starting from light industries when Korea exported merely 20 million dollar's worth of fishery products and tungsten.

In the beginning, international financing was more of a hope for Korea than a plan. No international financial institution wanted to lend money simply based on a guarantee from the Korean government whose foreign exchange reserves were close to zero. Korea sent trained nurses to German hospitals, and mine workers to mines to earn foreign exchange. Gen. Park who had become President Park visited West Germany to ask for financing for his projects on a rented commercial plane paid for by the West German government. At a public speech in front of the tired Korean nurses and mine workers he actually failed to control his surging emotion and cried with them hands-in-hand without any words for several minutes.

Korea also sent forty thousand combat soldiers to Vietnam to fight shoulder-to-shoulder with the US GIs. The monthly salary paid to the Korean soldiers, US$152[42] paid by the US government stacked up to a significant sum. But it was nowhere near enough to finance building the first Korean nonstop highway connecting Seoul and Busan, the largest port of Korea, and the Pohang Integrated Steel Mill. Korea even concluded a reparation agreement with Japan at 5 hundred million dollars, 200 million in free aid, and 300 million in commercial loans.[43]

The diplomatic relationship between Korea and Japan is never friendly. The majority of Japanese leaders think that there is no historical reason to apologize to Korea. The real

---

[42] "Study of the Overseas Allowance for Korean Combat Soldiers to Vietnam" by Yong Ho Choi, The Military History NO 58 April 2006.

[43] It is not compensation for the brutal damage caused by Japaneses government and corporations to the Korean civilians for 36 years including the attempt to wipe out Korean history, culture, and language, or forced sex slaves of Korean girls. The colonial exploitation lasted for 36 years. The agreement does not state any pardons for the sins of Japan. No democratic government in the world, including Korea, can receive money and pardon the guilt of the brutal colonial ruling on behalf of the sufferers, the people. People have right to demand admissions of guilt by the Japanese government anytime, anywhere which the Japanese government declines.

problem is that Japan's Ministry of Education has adopted only those textbooks that distort history denying the atrocities, or claiming that the Japanese government was not involved. The third-generation Japanese now firmly believe that the military sex slavery is a lie that Korea and China concocted, and Korea was the beneficiary of generous Japanese imperial rule. Japan is using its education system as a propaganda machine and turning its children into international misfits immersed in a globally incompatible culture with a false sense of history in the global community.

Foreign direct investment to Korea was a luxury that Korea was not blessed with. The World Bank organized the IECOK (International Economic Consultative Organization for Korea) to help Korea finance its development projects by inviting leading government treasuries and global financing institutions. The organization held annual meetings in major cities of the world. The first meeting was held in 1966 in Paris just before the commencement of the Second Five-Year Economic and Social Plan of Korea. The World Bank made a presentation on the results and appraisal of the first Five-Year Plan performance by Korea. The Korea Economic Planning Board representative presented the contents of the Second Plan and the financial resources required. Participants were given the opportunity to book high-return Korean bonds. The mechanism of economic development by borrowing was constructed this way.

## Unique Corporate Financing Strategy

Financing Korean economic development was the hardest part. At the end, after all those heated discussions and thick documents, it all came down to project financing for building production plants. POSCO and KEPCO (power company) were the few public companies built under the ownership of the government, and others were all privately owned.

Project financing by Korean corporations was a well-kept secret until this quiet money succeeded in creating large corporations in many industries. The thirty-some businessmen just released from prison for profiteering suddenly discovered that their new responsibility was to make good profits by executing the projects of the Five Year Plan. Failure in this new task could be jail again for it would be an unforgivable waste of valuable foreign capital. On the other hand, success in the first project guaranteed even bigger profit opportunities in new projects that were a hundred times harder. They didn't have to be ambitious for general Park was nothing if he was not ambitious. Reluctantly they became integral parts of the Korean developmental machine.

Corporate financing was generally kept within tight circles for it might have invited the attention of tax officers who had to meet the daily quota of finding unreported taxable income. Tax officers usually despair because the vaults of the Korean corporations were practically empty compared to the size of the investment projects allocated to them needed. Korean corporations were so poorly capitalized; they had to invent a Rule of 1/3. The first one-third came from foreign sources provided by the government-owned Korea Development Bank. The second third came from Korean domestic banks who lent money on the basis of Korean government guarantees. The last one third came from internal sources of the corporations. The stock market did not exist in Korea then.

At the completion of the first two five-year plans, most Korean corporations had two to four large companies under their wings controlled by a single owner. One group controlled a wool textile company, sugar refinery company, and international trading company, and wanted to build a urea plant. Another controlled an automobile repair plant, a decently successful construction, and engineering company, and wanted to build a dockyard for shipbuilding. Basically, all other company groups were in a similar situation. To garner the last one-third of the capital, they directed all the companies under their wing to borrow through second mortgages of any assets the companies possessed. The first mortgage was taken already by lenders at the beginning of the formation of the group.

One phone call from a senior officer of the Ministry of Finance to the president of the bank settled the whole problem. Actually, the presidents of commercial banks knew who needs how much money for their projects. At this stage, the CEOs of the urea company and the shipbuilding company, into which all the new capital will be channeled, were most likely negotiating for the land price to locate their plants, and seeking the availability of secondhand plant equipment and machines with American, German, and Japanese plant makers.

The final one-third of the capital was supposed to come from the internal resources of the company but Korean future giants simply did not have the money. Korea rewrote the dictionary to say that *internal* is the same as *intramural* and *domestic*. The shipbuilder spent the initial contract money, which was for building the first ship the company ever built, in constructing the dockyard for shipbuilding. The urea maker sold part of its equity shares to local urea distributors before plant construction began. Thus the Korean version of the government-industry coalition was created. From a macro point of view the extensive corruption that this system can entail was a minor abscess compared to the national achievement of the march to prosperity. The public hated the emerging Jaebols. They were so far ahead in wealth, opportunity, and international stature compared to the rest of the country, under the heavily biased love and favor from the military government. That was a poor man's solution to financing economic development projects.

# Over Borrowing and Adjustment

At times, corporations have to compete with each other when the source of funding is restricted by the government. Throughout the high growth period of the 70s to the early 90s, the Korean government monopolized the borrowing channel of foreign funds by designating the government-owned KDB as the single international financing window. This Development Bank, for over 30 years, practically rationed foreign funds to Korean industrial giants by prohibiting private companies from independently borrowing from foreign financial sources. I am one of the living witnesses. In the middle of the 1980s Samsung Corp was offered many lending opportunities by international lending institutions in terms and conditions much more favorable than the KDB's terms but we never got the approval from the government to borrow independently.

Like any economic restriction, this rigidity of the Korean government entailed generalized excessive competition among Korean corporations in the borrowing market, and this included back-door channels. All we had to do was to let our London office, which is registered as a British subject, borrow on behalf of the head office in Seoul, and Korean bureaucrats knew this but they turned their heads in the other direction. However, these bureaucrats never gave up their turf unless an enlightened higher officer coerced them to change the rules. Government restriction and bureaucratic greed for turf naturally breed immorality of excess competition, entailing over-borrowing and over-investment.[44]

So the money problem was resolved one way or another. The government practically wiped out meager Korean private sector capital through land reform, In order to supply capital for growth the government and the private sector did all they can, Naturally our international borrowing blew up in scale far beyond our ability to manage, and balance sheets of nearly all Korean companies started to loudly scream danger signals. Debt-equity ratios of most of Jaebol companies passed the 300% mark. We were crushed in the economic crisis with massive liquidations as

---

[44] That is immoral because people break rules, not because anybody plans not to pay them back. The famous stigma of *moral hazard* blames borrowers as if the borrower from the beginning planned to refuse to redeem. If it becomes impossible to pay back the bank debt, it is not a matter of morality. It is a stupidity of bad planning and bad management. If somebody borrows with an ntention not to pay back, it is not a moral hazard, it is a crime.

the international lending companies simultaneously pulled their short-term loans, financed by the yen-carry funds with near-zero interest, out of Korea on December 16, 1997. I hope other developing countries prepare for better options if they face a similar situation.

The crisis of overinvestment and the following adjustment in 1997 was painful with a lot of bloodsheds, and was very expensive.[45] Many admire the V-shaped recovery of Korea from a deep trough with a negative GDP growth of -5.6% to a real GDP growth rate of over 12% in a matter of one year. Compared to the L-shaped continuous sinking of Japan, which they call the lost thirty years, it was a notable achievement. But the real value of the crisis came from the pain itself. The general readjustment that accompanied many liquidations and M&As made the remaining survivors strong and competitive.

By 2021, to skip a little, with the crisis as tonic energizer Korean technology reached a point where it was the global leader in proprietary technologies of several impor-

---

[45] Ungsuh Kenneth Park, ibid. Enough has been written on the Korean economic crisis of 1997 and this book is one of them. Out of 30 largest corporate groups, only 13 survived and still going on strong, but the rest either closed or changed ownership.

tant industries including semiconductor memory; systems chip fabrication, LNG carriers powered by LNG engines, hydrogen-powered trucks and engines, and safe lithium batteries.

Samsung Electronics, a semiconductor memory chip company, started in the summer of 2022 mass production of 3 nanometer transistors based on GAA (gate all around) technology for the first time in the world. The system chip-design capability of this memory chip company entices great CPU-APU makers like QUALCOMM, Nvidia, IBM, and AMD to agree on joint design projects for new-generation CPUs for computers, GPUs for graphics, APUs for mobile phones, and MCUs for automobiles. Samsung recently announced that the company succeeded in developing *CPU In-memory*, a memory with CPU on it, that substantially reduces the von Neumann Bottleneck problem.[46] President Biden understands that the global balance of the semiconductor supply depends on Korean chip makers and repeatedly invites them to White House and encourages Korean lithium battery makers and chip makers to invest in America.[47]

---

[46] In computer architecture, the speed of computation cannot exceed what is allowed to pass through by the throughput capacity of the data channel between the CPU and Memory. This is called the won Neumann bottleneck.

[47] TSMC, an OEM fabricator of system chips takes pride in their policy that it never competes against its client, insinuating that Samsung competes against Qualcom's

Two critical bottlenecks still waited for us. The first was proprietary *technology* owned by the most advanced companies in the world in HMPE industries. The second is the lack of *experience* by Korean corporations in the new HMPE industries. For success in this game technology and responsible organizations are as important as capital. The way Korea handled these two bottlenecks put Korea on an entirely different trajectory that is full of risk and probabilities of failure. Other dragons took safer roads. We will see how Korea resolved the question of technology in the next chapter, and will examine the question of the industrial organization of the major corporations in the chapter after next.

---

Snapdragon in APU market with its own Exynos. As the semiconductor demand is going to explode in the AI revolution era supported by 5th and 6th generation telecommunication, remaining as an commissioned outside producer can be a dangerous strategy. OEM manufacturers can pop up all over the world especially in America. US government is encouraging it to Samsung, SK, TSMC, and many others. Concentrating on commissioned manufacturing suits well in pre-corona world, but in post-corona economy the power rises in original designs, not original equipment manufacturing (OEM), for imagination is the only limit for inventing new ways to make use of AI and wide and efficient connectivity, and larger part of it comes in the form of new designs of extended realities. Commissioned producer falls into a paradoxical trap that comes from the comfort of being relieved from worrying about the future. That is the role of fabless designers of semiconductors and the systems. Fab owners will be several steps behind the fabless designers.

# VIII. Technology Nationalism

## Japan's Lost 30 Years

The worship of perfect workmanship provided industrial success in Japan until the beginning of the 1990's when the bubble started to burst led by the real estate price collapse in Tokyo. The Bank of Japan raised the interest rate by just one per cent, and that was enough to trigger a chain reaction of a downward spiral of property prices. They were so used to a near-zero interest rate for decades, that even one a percent interest rate charged by the central bank drove the entire economy into a downward spiral. Near zero interest was the very lynch pin that prevented domestic inflation even with the massive inflow of the dollar through chronic structural balance-of-payment surpluses, which in turn was maintained by the policy of keeping a cheap and under-valued yen. Four decades of a massive trade surplus made Japan the largest dollar reserve country in the world until China took over.[48]

Raising the yen value by close to 100 % (from 230 yen to a dollar to 110 yen to a dollar) by the pressure of trading partners, called the Plaza Accord, and raising the prime interest rate to 1% demolished the clever combination of cheap yen and zero interest and drove the country into three decades of stagnation. If the excessive exports were due to their superior technology and productivity of Japanese corporations, the massive liquidity injection by Mr. Abe should have caused an equally massive investment but the real growth rate stayed near zero for three decades. Japanese corporations could have used the opportunities given by the easy money policy for their corporate reforms and technological innovations, but they wasted the chance. When corporate profits shrank with the long recession, the Japanese labor unions proudly demanded wage reductions and the aggregate demand shrank for 30 years.

While blaming the central bank and government, the corporate sector was comfortably exempted from the blame

---

[48] Economists call the forcing excessive dollar out of country by keeping the interest very low or zero as *sterilizing* the economy from the germs of inflation.

of economic stagnation, and they continued indulging in *doing the same thing* over three decades. In the obsession to perfection of existing product technology and the production process, they lost touch with the market, which demanded new products with new technology such as OLED TV and monitors, electric and self-driving cars, mobile telephones with memory capacity matching major university computer centers 40 years ago, 5th Generation tele-communication systems that require semiconductors which can compute 5 trillion bits per second, 100 million pixel cameras, etc. These are the very new technologies Japanese corporations refused to develop while Korean corporations found them as the chance to surpass Japanese counterparts. By refusing to shed the old technology and develop and embrace new technology and industry, Japanese corporations violated the cardinal rule of industrial migrations and took Japan out of the international value chain system. The poor Korean companies had to seek for the international markets for their new products because their domestic market was small, but the lucky Japanese companies had larger domestic market waiting for their products. Does it remind the Chinese leader, Xi, Jin Ping?

Young Japanese bloggers complained in SNSs, 'Who needs world's safest trouble-free fax machine, when people all over the world use email and cloud service?' Japanese corporate leaders believed that they should stay within their turf in which they are the best in the world, meanwhile the world had discarded the turf altogether. The speed of introducing new markets for new products has doubled 5 times in the 21$^{st}$ century compared to the 20$^{th}$ century according to Ray Kurzweil, the famous American scientific futurologist.[49]

For far too long Japan took pride in being the world's best number two after the Au Bey Sen Shin Goku (Euro-American Advanced Countries). The Japanese government applied for membership in the EU, and the EU dismissed the request instantly. Perfecting existing product and production technologies provided Japan with good wealth and there was no reason to kill the goose that laid golden eggs. But the golden eggs are turning into rocks. No

[49] To be fair to the science community of Japan, it must be mentioned that the country somehow entered into a limping stage in science and technology. While conservative industries are slowing down the Japanese economy, the space industry community roars ahead at a strong and healthy speed. Japan is second to the USA in creating the Space Command which promises to be one of the new sources of military power in the not so distant future. In sweeping space debris Japan is one of the leaders of the world.

Euro-American companies are willing to disclose advanced original technologies to Japan or anyone. They are not for sale, period. That's where Koreans departed from the Japanese model of building a technology base that would last for centuries.

The Chinese communist government decided to steal whatever technology they needed and the ingenuity in setting up the system of theft of foreign technology does not need repetition here. They developed a unique legal-scientific mechanism that mobilizes 1.4 billion people in and out of China and coerces students and ordinary workers to steal very tiny part of new technologies, and the thief does not know the purpose. Like mindless robots they had to steal as they were required to by law, and instructed to do by the party. But at least China did not slow down. If anything China as a whole is more frantic and scared of being left behind than Korea.

For Korea to catch up with the most advanced rich economies of the world, acceleration of Korean technology progress was not enough. Front runners have the advantage of better tools for research invented by the most advanced research institutes. We are developing technologies but they are researching scientific principles and theories. The race is not fair and the rules of market competition apply in technology world more tightly.

Everybody says that the 21$^{st}$ century is the age of digital technology. We were happily proselytized, and the entire Peninsula is connected wirelessly with internet WiFi and data transmission network. Once connected, new ideas and opportunities for fusion came automatically. Even for a simple farmer, every day turned into a challenge of connecting the urban consumers with his fresh delivery through his digital site run by the cooperative to which he belongs. Opportunities are equally available to everybody and if your neighbor's produce is picked up by a truck from a nationwide logistics company while your produce is still in the field waiting for you to pick it, you have nobody else to blame but yourself.

Believe me we never cursed Europe or prayed for their slow down, but they did slow down. They seem to be in some sort of stupor of systematized income redistribution agenda, or suffering from some hallucination of subsidized prosperity. The new world of techno-digital space and a limitless number of meta-verses are waiting for our colonization. This time our colonization efforts will receive no resistance and meet no human rights problems. And the resources are limitless for the size is determined by our imagination. But corporations from rich countries seem to have tied themselves to the old ways of doing things. Where are the European Elon Musks and Steve Jobs? We are about to enter a world where billions of electronic goods and vehicles for transportation are equipped with computers and communication devices each sending out trillions of bits of data and responding to each other. We will visit this subject when we discuss the future of Korean economy. The concept of prosperity may have to change in a hyper-connected world.

## Improvement versus Innovation

Not many know the Japanese word "*Kaisen*". It is literarily *improvement* in Japanese and many books are written about Kaisen in the Japanese language, and they were translated into many other languages. It became sort of a symbol of management victory of Japanese corporations over Americans. It embodies the spirit of endless improvement in product designs and production process technology. If an individual or a team fails to come up with additional improvement in the quality and durability as well as cutting production costs, the guilty party is subjected to public humility, reflecting the ugly side of the communitarian culture where individual failures are regarded as the cause of embarrassment to the community or state, and such embarrassment should be prevented, in some cases, by an honorable suicide.

This worship for Kaisen is a result of Japanese ingenuity in their discovery of the difference between product technology and production technology. The *product life-cycle theory* taught in the US management schools is based on the rise and fall of the sales of a product, measured both in changes of sales volume and profitability. According to this theory when both sales and profit of a product start to shrink, the company is advised to dispose of it courageously, and focus limited corporate resources on products that will render better returns. That will create another legend of a great success like Apple and Tesla or

Ford and GE a century ago.

This managerial wisdom proved correct as long as there are many alternative new products with new technologies available in the product and technology portfolio of the company. This is precisely the strategy that made America the pioneer of products such as electric power, automobiles, household electronics, semiconductors, internet network protocols, robotics, mobile phones, artificial intelligence, MMORPG, and unmanned vehicles. Time and resources should be allocated to the industry and product with the highest potential returns, not the old declining dinosaurs (mature products). Besides over eighty percent of the markets for the products of major US companies are inside the USA, which is the market for the best and most advanced products. Serving the rest of the world with mature old products takes a very low priority in American companies.

On the other hand, Europe and Japan were several steps behind the USA in the game of introducing entirely new products and creating new markets. For them, the best strategy was searching the waste baskets containing product portfolios of American companies to improve upon them. This is the time when the USA had 40% of the global GDP from the end of WWII to the first oil shock of 1972. American multinational companies started to overwhelm European and Japanese companies and the ghost of Euro-pessimism prevailed over them. The trade liberalization process of GATT[50] reached the Kennedy Round which gave access to the massive US market for the products of any other countries.

Fortunately for the Europeans and Japanese, the US products at the end of their life cycle left a huge gap not served in mature markets. Color TVs, videos equipment, CDs, washing machines, dryers, refrigerators, cars, small trucks, vans, cameras, H- beams of steel, and cargo ships were no longer profitable for the American companies to continue producing in the USA. That was the cleavage for the Kaisen strategy to fill. The international competitors with lower domestic wages improved on not only the quality of these mature products, but more importantly, they systematically improved the production processes.

---

[50] General Agreement of Tariff and Trade, forerunner of the WTO, set up at the end of WWII together with the commencement of the Unite Nations.

When this author was appointed as the executive vice president of Samsung Electronics Company in 1984, an insignificant household electronics assembly company then, my first visit to the plant at Suwon started at the Production Technology Research Center, which was a new term for me. The research staff was busy with topics such as robotic delivery of components to the right places at the right time for workers, or designing rolled-up tape that is glued with ceramic conductors, diodes, capacitors and semiconductors to be inserted in the right holes of green printed circuit boards (PCB) automatically at high speed. This is the production technology which was invented by the second tier competitors, Japan and Germany.

The massive markets of mature products such as color televisions, which more than hundred companies could produce all over the world, the profit margins were near zero. To sustain the business with some profit, costs should be reduced by high speed production and delivery, with the highest productivity per worker, and high quality and durability of products. This explains why American business schools teach better marketing and M&A courses, and Asian business schools teach better supply strategy and cost management courses. All the companies outside America were playing the game of Kaisen.

This blind worship of 'improvement' made Japan the second largest and Germany the third largest economies in the world. I am yet to be convinced that the large number of Nobel laureates from these countries directly helped to increase corporate bottom lines. The number of patents applied for and granted to a country, and the number of companies listed on the Fortune 500 are strongly correlated, but economic growth rates and the Nobel prizes earned by countries seem inversely correlated. Why?

## History of Catching UP by Technology Nationalism

Technology was mainly stored in human brains and in written documents before the computer was invented, and when people with technological knowledge moved from one place to other, technology, and prosperity followed with them. One good visible example is the unusual location of a church called Franzosiche Kirche, literally the

French Church. It is located in the middle of Friedrichstadt Strasse in Berlin, among German royal palaces, a university, and museums such as Pergamum. In front of the church building there is a metal plaque showing an engraved picture of French Huguenots bowing to the king Friedrich who granted the land and materials to build the church. The king welcomed the protestant Huguenots for they came with new technology, escaping the persecution by the catholic French government. They fled France to England, Netherland, protestant Belgium, and Germany, which were the cradles of the first Industrial Revolution.

When Turkey was occupied by an Islam state, ending the Byzantine rule, and the Silk Road was shut down, Anatolian masters and craftsmen migrated to Northern Italy in massive numbers and opened the door of the Renaissance. What a contrast to the present Syrian refugees. The massive movement of the Huguenots after the Reformation, the war between churches, caused the creation of a new map for the distribution of wealth among European countries. The most recent mass movement of scientists and technicians happened when the US-Soviet military rushed to capture the city of Berlin at the end of WWII, where most of the great

German scientists and technicians lived. Soviets captured the scientists forcefully and Americans invited them to America with generous gift and the chance for continuous research work. Thus the space race began, they say. They represent the fully recorded history of policies reflecting the underlying technology nationalism.

Technology nationalism is not widely used term although it was the main avenue of competition, and it is the key indicator of success/failure in the Cold War between the West and the Soviet Block.. In the end Mr. Gorbachev, then Soviet Prime Minister, had to initiate his Perestroika (Restructuring) and Glasnost(Open Economy) that marked the end of Cold War when he realized that the Soviet-side was defeated because of Star Wars, the missile interception technology developed by the USA. The MAD (Mutually Assured Devastation) doctrine was the underlying basis of the equilibrium of terror and the Anti-ballistic missile treaty(A promise not to develop missile interception technology) between USA and the Soviet Union. But this US missile interception technology (the Star War of Reagan) instantly made this doctrine useless.

But there is one more fairly large movement of scientists from a falling country. When the Soviet Union fell to pieces in early 1990s, there was a substantial movement of Russian scientists.[51] Samsung as a group invited a substantial number of Russian scientists for which there is no data. So did other Korean corporations.[52]

Blue laser technology was one important technology for semiconductors that Samsung obtained through this channel. When Yeltzin's Russia declared a moratorium on foreign debt, most of western corporations departed the new Russia, for the recovery seemed so far away, but major Korean Jaebols remained and helped with the recovery process. Korea even lent 1.47 billion US dollars to the government of Mr. Gorbachev, which needed hard currency badly. The new Russia took over the liability in its entirety. That turned into a stroke of genius, and the subsequent

---

[51] I personally had a series of visits at my office in Seoul by Russian middle men who wanted to sell Russian technology from the end of 1980s to early 1990s. Some of them wanted to sell stolen Russian plutonium which I declined. But I did invite five Russian scientists to work at our chemical research center for development of a new catalyst while I paid for their families' travel to the US and for the university education of their children.

[52] Although there was nothing to export to the chaotic markets of Moscow, which had virtually no foreign exchanges to spend, I routinely encountered the senior executives of LG, SK, Hyundai, etc. at the corridors of Bolshoi and Stanislavsky opera houses. Whom we met during the day, we closed our mouths.

Russian government is still paying the debt back in kinds, mainly with the most advanced Russian tanks and missiles. They know Korea is excellent in reverse engineering. When weapons have American proprietary technology and US made components, we have to get the permission from American government, but when we export weapons using Russian technology, Moscow is silent. So far.

When a country invests in HMPE industries on a massive scale, it is automatically planning to export the products. The domestic market simply does not have enough need for them. Even if there is a huge domestic market like in China, a plan is required that will provide a scale of investment large enough for exports in order to get dollars for raw material and component imports. In other words, there is no room for HMPE products with quality lower than the international standard because everybody in this industry exports. That demands latest and best technology in each industry. If there is any technology transfer, it will take place with strict restrictions that prevents the recipients from competing with the donor. The latest technology of a company that survives in this tough market elicits national pride for the country. In other words, this technology nationalism is the key strategy for the successful entry into HMPE industries and into rich countries. There is no generous fool in this industry. Imagine supersonic jet fighters designed and manufactured by your own engineers fly in the sky and gets exported. It is just as exciting as winning at a World Cup soccer game.

## Foreign Investment and Technology Transfer

In inviting American, European and Japanese engineers who possessed advanced technology, as well as the corporate managers, to come and work with domestic engineers and scientists, Korea was the worst choice. For the potential visitors bringing their families to live and educating their children in local international schools, Korea was not an attractive option. Psychologically, to potential visitors, Korea is located at the end of the (free) world with its demilitarized zone and North Korean hostile long-range artillery and nuclear bombs aiming right at their back. Korea's high-quality workforce and low wages among the dragons did not help to improve the insignificant foreign direct investment statistics as shown in the previous tables.

If technological assistance by the corporations and scientists of advanced countries were to be the only source of technologies and scientific information, Korea should have been the last dragon to join the OECD, the club consisting of the 30 richest countries. But it broke the wall first before any other dragons. For the same reason Korea should have been the last dragon to be invited to the G7 Summit. The fact that Korea is invited to the G7 meetings is a form of international recognition that Korea is important enough to consult with in dealing with the common problems of peace, prosperity, and individual freedom of humanity. This is an absolute paradox. Korea still is the same small remote place under threat of war with harsh weather conditions resided in by people who shy away from visitors when approached, for many of them don't understand questions in English.

Among all the paradoxes, shattering the technology paradox was the hardest of them all to Korea. Engineering schools in Hong Kong and Singapore used English as a means of communication and many high-quality scientists enjoyed the invitation to visit the campuses of these semitropical island countries. Quickly the international ratings of several of these universities rose at a phenomenal speed. Taiwan universities that spoke the same mother tongue as the students and faculties of famous Hong Kong universities couldn't escape the favorable intellectual tide of influence. Korean universities were isolated again and they had to get whatever they needed by themselves.

There were several channels through which foreign technology, mainly from Japan, flew into the Korean workshops and plants. The Friday night moon shined on planes to and from Tokyo and Osaka to Seoul, Busan, Ulsan, and Suwon carrying Japanese technology advisors, and these engineers were paid quite generously. Visits to Japanese manufacturing plants gave excellent education opportunities to Korean plant and machine design engineers.

Many of the technologies came through the channel of technology transfer contracts that required paying expensive royalties, but this knowledge was simple, and mostly on operating expensive machines imported with some basic repair skills and information. With this practice, Korean corporations could never surpass the Japanese and would have remained as a disposable part of the value chain system ruled by Japanese companies.

Thirty years later, Samsung Electronics Co. departed the City of Hui Jou where it used to manufacture smart phones to supply the China market. Now, local competitors sell the smart phones at less than half the price of Samsung's phones with the support of a Chinese government subsidy. Samsung simply discarded the real estate and built a new facility in Bhac Nin Province near Hanoi, Vietnam, where it now produces semiconductor memory and mobile phones worth one quarter of Vietnam's GDP. Samsung left China because the wage level of Vietnam guaranteed higher profit than China. The mighty China became a humble disposable component of the Samsung Empire of semiconductor and smart phone manufacturing.

As long as Korea continued to rely on Japanese technology, the future was as clear as the writing on the wall. Korea needed a technology strategy that did not depend on the decisions of investors and technology providers. Without an independent system that could acquire the most advanced technologies, even a great country like China would become merely a disposable part of the global value-chain system ruled by the hub companies. Mr. Trump and Mr. Biden are jointly proving that.

## The Korean Model of Technology Nationalism

The Korean model can be summed up in two words, 'Technology Nationalism.' Koreans stole too. The story of the Friday night Japanese technical migrants who moonshined in Korea over the weekends became a legend now. But if that was all, then Korea would never have technologically surpassed Japan. The best of Japanese scientists and engineers wouldn't visit Korea over weekends and earn a few dollars. For technological independence the Korean scientists and engineers should be better than their Japanese counterparts in their own fields.

Technological Independence of the industries of a country can be defined as possessing the (1) the ability to design new final products as well as the manufacturing process relying on local and foreign expert scientists and engineers, (2) the ability to produce a product in high enough quality and a low enough cost to sell in the international markets, and (3) the ability to nurture domestic component, material and equipment industries that can supply more than 70% of the requirement. But in practical terms, the technological independence of a country will show up in the performance and quality of the products in actual use. If it is disappointing, then soon consumers will depart. Professor Michael Porter of Harvard Business School sums up this concept as the Competitive Advantage in his numerous publications. Ability to invent a new product is not enough to provide technology independence. Numerous other factors that give to the product the advantages to dominate the market constitute as a whole shows the technology independence.

Korea now is technologically independent in producing and exporting 5th generation telecommunication equipment and networks, ranking one of the largest in the world.[53] Korea controls over 75% of the semiconductor memories market, and fabricates neural processing units (NPU) for Qualcom, AMD and NVidia, using 3 to 4 Nano meter EUV (Extreme Ultra Violet) processing technology.

---

[53] Huawei used to be the largest but quickly shrank by US governmental prohibitions and China-decoupling policy.

It is the global leader of hydrogen-electricity vehicles as well as the lithium battery industry by controlling 70% of the market, and 96% of QLED and OLED display industry.

There are no statistics that show the technological independence of industries by country. People frequently use the international patent statistics to measure the state of the technological development of a country. A country's ranking in patent applications as an indicator of the level of technology is misleading. The collective scientific and technical intellect of any country can be much bigger than what the patent application ranking shows. Besides, one country may lead in micro-biological and medical research but its overall ranking in patents may be low because the country may concentrate its resources in what it can do best.

With that in mind, in the international patents in 2020, US companies applied for 226,297 patents, followed by Japan with 195,906 patents, Germany with 99,791 patents, China with 96,268 patents, and Korea with 80,133 patents. That makes Korea one of the top five patent applicants for the international protection of their technology and knowhow. There are 15.9 million patents in force and under protection by WIPO, the World Intellectual Property Organization. Among them 3.3 million patents belong to US companies, 3.1 million to China, 2 million to Japan, 1.1 million to Korean and 0.8 million to German companies. These statistics show the past accumulation of technologies worthy of protection hence any new super star in patent applications cannot be included here. In other words, Korea was and is one of the top five countries in inventing/ developing new technologies that need protection for quite some time.

There is no Nobel Prize for technological achievement. It is for great scientific discoveries. The information in the articles published in great journals is free, and anybody can repeat an experiment to confirm. But technology is a valuable intellectual property that is patented and protected from duplication without permission. Although a good national technology strategy cannot exist without an excellent science strategy, what we directly need for economic development is technology, and the corporate technology strategy is more important than any university science strategy at the beginning. Technological excellence of the major domestic corporations brought in prosperity and the ability to sustain economic growth.

The first part of the Korean technology strategy was *"Start the process from building a technology base rather than science base"*. This is poor man's solution, for this path brings income quicker than broad science-based approach. Basic science is too broad but technology can be sharply focused in a selected few industries. LG[54] was the first Korean technological company producing low-quality radios and transistors from 1950's. Purely by responding to market demand it kept on investing in technology and has now become the global leader in OLED displays, rollable TV, and lithium batteries. Samsung in the fifties refined raw sugar that was given in aid to the Korean government by the US AID. Inspired by the great Japanese electronics companies Samsung Electronics was established in 1968. It has now become the leader in memory semiconductors and the leader in system on chips HBM, High-Bandwidth Memory, or Hybrid Bonded Memory. SK Hynix, another Korean memory company ranking third in the world in memory supply, developed the HBM first and Samsung

---

[54] Lucky-Gold Star is abbreviated into LG and it started with tooth paste and radios. But LG was technologically the most advanced company in Korea in1950s.

joined right after. They are only companies in the world capable of designing and producing the CPU-on-Memory chips that will someday make the traditional independent CPUs useless.

We absorbed the technology of advanced countries like sponges whenever there were opportunities. We took technology from the USA, Japan, and Europe even from the Soviets who were officially our national enemy. Technology Nationalism became corporate culture in Korean companies. But imported technology can never give technology independence. As we will see soon our domestic technology demand was sharply focused and whatever was not available for buying our scientists developed the technology domestically.

The second strategy for our technological independence was *"Leave it to the private companies."* The reward for market-oriented technology growth is called the technology instrumentalism in Korea. This concept will be discussed more deeply in the next section. As the economic growth approached the mature industrial stage, this strategy of object-oriented technology research development proved very useful. The great Korean corporations and their supplier network envisage the changing needs of the market three to five years ahead, and the amateur public servants who continually rotated their positions, could never compete against the experts of industry. When companies predict the future market demand five years in advance, and prepare for the future both technologically and financially, bureaucrats of both democratic and communist governments cannot compete with the private sector professionals. Inaccurate predictions and bets could entail a waste of billions of dollars.

Almost automatically our engineers started to dismantle the machines and equipment. They had to know why a particular machine works to produce its intended product. The penalty was stiff. As soon as they took the machine apart, all the warranties disappeared. Many international equipment suppliers declined to make deals with us after such incidents. They insulted us harshly. But our engineers succeeded in rebuilding and repairing the machines, and eventually they cracked the full details of the principles and mechanics of the machine. They reinvented and gave new meanings to the concept of, *reverse engineering*. Once the stiff penalty is paid, we are left with the principal scientific knowledge related to the product, production, and maintenance. Eventually our engineers started to improve on the original machines, and submitted their superior improvements for patent protection.

Soon our engineers found that the components of the reinvented machines were not for sale. This is called Bupoom and the abbreviated version is the Bu problem. Furthermore, the material that the components used was unique and patented by small unknown companies in the remote Scandinavian or German countryside. This material supply is called Sojae, or the So problem. That is not all. Frequently either the components, material or the final products required new equipment and machines that fabricate the materials or manipulate the feed stocks properly. It is called Jangchi, or the Jang problem. Altogether we call these concepts the Sobujang problem.

Abe Shinzo, former prime minister of Japan implemented a new regulation in 2019 under which all the Sobujang for semiconductor manufacturing should be approved item by item every time they get exported to Korea. The Korean politicians, who normally would never agree on anything with their opposition parties, admirably passed new laws that provide easy financial access to the small and medium Sobujang companies, domestic or foreign. Korean corporations that produce the final products, semiconductors, started to assist their Sobujang satellite companies with free access to their technology, and paid the Sobujang in advance for services/products under development.

Foreign investors rapidly filled this market vacated by Japan and took advantage of Korean government assistance. Material science, component manufacturing mechanics, and technology for designing equipment are usually left to advanced country suppliers. This vertically complementary division of labor is a vital frame, under which the global value chain system continues to develop. The sobujang technology is not limited to semiconductors. At any level of technological progress, a developing country was never required a technological self-sufficiency of intermediate products for the *entire range*, for the world is nicely networked in a supply chain of competitive advantages. But the suicidal act of Mr. Abe took Japan out of this chain of supply, for nobody will expose themselves to the danger of arbitrary and abrupt supply ban by a long term contract with Japanese companies any more. Technologically advanced economies do not use technological dependence of their clients as a weapon of aggression. He altered the international trade into a weapon.

What the government of Japan did was equivalent to decoupling its industries from the global supply chain. Korea should be thankful to Mr. Abe for giving a chance to perfect its own scientific base of supply industries for the semiconductor. Japan used to produce high quality Sobujang at the best prices, and Korea happily relied on their supply. But he practically killed the excellent Japanese industry in one stroke. He must have forgotten that Korea supplies three quarters of the global memory market therefore is the life-supporting line to Japan's Sobujang makers. Abe aimed to get more votes to Jiminto Party by leveling a deadly blow to Samsung and SK semiconductor companies, and semiconductors are the largest single Korean export item. His blow killed several Japanese Sobujang companies instead, but Japanese voters still overwhelmingly vote for the Jiminto Party.

The utilitarian market-oriented technology development strategy, however, leaves a product-related research culture and creates an extremely narrow and biased technology and science ecology. In the short run it may be the only option to a beginner of economic development, but as the industrialization gets mature, we needed better-balanced science research and education ecology.

## History of Government-Funded Research

When Korea started as an independent nation, the government began mandatory education and forcefully redistributed the ownership of all farmlands to serfs and tenants. In 1950 just a few months before the war, Korea established the first government-funded research institute named the Science-Technology Institute of National Defense. The founding fathers understood that the engine for economic growth and national development comes out of science and technology. That was just the beginning.

In the spring of 1965, when President Chung Hee Park met President Lyndon Johnson in Washington, they agreed that the US government would assist in establishing a science and technology institute with funds, personnel and knowhow.[55] President visited the KIST (Korea Institute of Science and Technology) on average twice a month for three years and enjoyed modest dinners with Makkoly, a popular local commoner's alcohol with the Korean scientists of the institute according to one of the young recruits. In May the same year he met a Korean electronics engineer with Penn State PhD degree at the Plaza Hotel New York city, and from that time persistently persuaded him to return to Korea. Dr. Kim, Gi Hyung returned and served as a member of the Presidential Council of Science and Technology, where he designed the Ministry of Science and Technology and he became the first minister. His ministry was the technological instrument in the successful construction and operation of the POSCO Steel Mill and the Wolsung Nuclear Power Plants for which Korea had no prior experience. According to the scientists of KIST and Dr. Kim, President Park never said no to their proposals. Science and technology was the key to his strategy of Leap-Frogging in industrial development.

---

[55] President Park established KIST[55] at the bottom of a small mountain known as the Forestry Testing Campus and recruited 20 Korean scientists from mainly American universities.

Clearly in President Park's mind, and in the thoughts of the people of Korea, science in general, and technology in particular, was an *instrument* for national development. The young recruits saw and knew what the advanced university labs and research institutes of America were doing. From their perspective, there were only two classes of countries; those who had particular scientific knowledge and those who did not. Since the young Korean scientists had the knowledge, all they have to do is, they thought, to transplant their American labs to Korea. They became the idealistic beacons of Korean science and technology policy, and this stimulated strong resistance from the local academic scientists. The idealists believed that Korea could become a G7 member in the global science and technology race. They actually achieved this goal in the Nuclear Power Plant technology. On the other hand one graduate from computer science department of a regional university confessed to me at a recruitment interview that he *did not see* a computer. This was in the late 1980s. This biased love of imported non-university institute scientists through government funding created a serious problem that took nearly a half century to resolve.

Up until the early 1970s, when Korea jumped into the HMPE industries, the research funds allocated to the universities was less than 1/10 of total government science and technology funding. The focus of the government funding policy was the transplantation of the advanced science and technology of rich countries to Korea in the shortest possible time. The young guns were square pegs in square holes for this purpose. But university professors were either trained in the pre-WWII Japanese universities, or they were their assistants who tended to repeat what their old teachers did. It took more than two decades for the scientists trained in the Western universities to replace majority of the old-school academics. President Park tried to circumvent this wall of old school by short circuiting it, and this tactic worked.

But this cleaver instrumentalism of science and technology comes with its own inherent problem. The 70s to Korea was a genesis period for HMPE industries. Technological instrumentalism provided the knowledge to design and produce advanced industrial goods very well. It even supplied the knowhow to improve upon the existing products or production methods. To clarify the problem let me explain the case of Chinese LCD technology. This liquid-crystal display technology is the most efficient and cheap image-displaying technology. By massive government subsidies, cheap production costs from low wages, and clever engineering, China's LCD makers wiped out the Japanese and Korea LCD makers. Up to this point, technology instrumentalism had worked well.

But that was not the end of the Korean and Japanese companies. LED, the light emission diodes gave the answer. In LCD technology, back-light panels receive the digital information to be shown on TVs and monitors, and repeat turning on-off switches that control pixels, while the frontal panels with three basic colors turn the lights into color images. In LED, each million diodes emit light in colors by the digital information it receives. Therefore it can be extremely thin and bendable. Japanese companies gave up this challenge and Korean companies succeeded in making marketable LED displays and now occupy 95% of the world market.

Japanese engineers said that it would be easier to climb Mount Fuji standing on your arms than for Korean engineers to succeed in developing LED displays. Jumping to the new LED technology requires a pool of advanced science in electronics, optics, organic chemistry, semiconductors, and new materials. Technology instrumentalism came into action here. The Ministry of Science and Technology invites the support of government-funded research institutes as well as private corporate research centers. Participants join in this huge research task by taking up parts where one has the advantage. And it worked by achieving specific big scale national goals. Korean technology instrumentalism served better in market competition.

But in order to discover an entirely new industry to lead the nation by generating new employment and investments, a country needs a wider and deeper personnel pool of people with knowledge in basic science. The broader pool of scientific information and talents needs to be developed without immediate uses. That's the sector the Korean government had long neglected. Technological instrumentalism quickly hit its limit and the policy focus had to take more balance. As a result, the government-funded Korea Basic Science Institute was hurriedly established.

But the country hit a new hurdle. As China virtually wiped out the cheaper end of all the HMPE industries, and Japan and Western companies occupied all the markets of the upper end of this industry, we were virtually cracked by the nutcracker of China at the bottom and Japan on top. We chose to challenge the upper end of the markets of each HMPE, and we found out that the Basic Science has the key. This was when our GDP per capita had reached just over USD 10,000; Korea was a comfortable middle-income country. Our graduates started to prefer white-color jobs and managerial positions that looked easier, than the plant managerial positions. At the beginning of the new millennia, a new social campaign began with the slogan, "The Shortage of a Science Workforce is a National Crisis." Blue color wage compensation rose nationwide, and the quality of engineering and science teaching rose remarkably. A network of new technological research institutes bloomed and job opportunities for PhDs in science became far easier.

The problem was not over yet. We did not know that there are two kinds of basic science until we discovered that what we called basic science was directly or indirectly related to the national or corporate objectives at that time. University scientists demanded funding for pure basic science such as Mathematical Science, Physics, Basic Chemistry, whereas the basic science centers planned for specific projects in Basic Engineering, and Radiation Beam Acceleration. This time the politicians started to take advantage of democracy. Korea did not receive any Nobel Prizes in Science and the public was persuaded to agree to finance the pure basic science projects to boost the road to this prize. If Koreans continued to fail in being awarded this prize, they know whom to blame.

## Slow Birth of a System

For egoistical reasons Samsung Electronics Co. (SEC) provides advanced notification with blue prints of the future products to the satellite companies to start developing required components, materials and equipment several years in advance. Naturally the product technology development centers of SEC and the satellites were tied up closely, and mutually fed each other important information on market trends along with technology at every stage of the development process. Any delay in the development of required parts and components, or inadequate quality and durability of components by supplier could wreck the whole project and the financial damage could be atronomical. The early exchange of information about the problems and troubles in the joint research process proved to be of immense value, and early adjustments of research parameters and requirements by all participants virtually assured the success.

At the beginning, the sheer need for a cheap and stable domestic supply system for critical components by Korean electronics companies forced the final product companies (FPC) and suppliers to cooperate with each other in building and securing an import substitution industry for Sobujang. The quality, durability, performance, and attraction of any final products could not surpass the limitations set by the same attributes of components. The day a shabby component breaks down is the day that the final product stops working. To beat the best in the world, the Korean Sobujang industry had to use the best materials, gadgets, and designs, with performance that our competitors could not match. That frequently required scientific discovery important enough to occupy the cover story of such journals as *Nature* and *Cell*.

When the FPC had to challenge the best in the world, the Sobujang system had to be supported by coordinated systems of research that could develop new materials and new energy sources, and extreme ultraviolet (EUV) lithography equipment that could handle 2 to 4 nanometer circuits. The supplier-FPC joint research system had to draw globally outstanding small companies into the coordinated research systems. Discovering small component makers with world class technology in small country towns of Germany, Netherland, Sweden, Estonia, Japan, etc. and commissioning them to make first-ever high tech components became a normal practice, and only this advanced global supply-chain system of high technology could introduce prize-winning new products that the world had never seen. With the limited population and technology base of Korea, this was the only way to compete against the American giants.

The second and equally important research system was created by the government-led target research projects. Just as major US corporations submit development plans of new-concept weapons to DARPA of the US Department of Defense, Korean major corporations and their first tier satellites frequently join in consortia with domestic university research institutes, relevant university departments, and government-funded research institutes to jointly apply for the money allocated to the new weapons development program. Hanhwa Systems, Hanhwa Defense (Former Samsung Precision Mechanics), LG Chemical, LG Energy Systems, LIG Signals, Korea Aerospace Industries (KAI), Hyundai Mobis, Hyundai Rotem, Hyundai Ship Building, and Samsung Heavy Industries are typical companies that exhibited powerful research capabilities in weapons development systems for land, sea, and air including AESA radar. Daewoo Shipbuilding (now Hanhwa Oceans) and Hyundai Heavy Industries, and Samsung Heavy Industries have demonstrated phenomenal growth recently by supplying naval medium-size carriers, submarines, and hypersonic missiles, stealth jet fighters, under-water ram-jet torpedoes with sonic speed, as well as LNG carrier tankers and LNG-powered ships that take practically 100% of the current global market.

Mr. Young Min Yoo was the Minister of Science, Technology and IT in the retiring administration.[56] In this period of industrial transition from one based on capital-labor to one based on knowledge-information, he defined the role of the government to be 'discovering the next set of bread-and-butter industries to generate employment and economic growth'. He is a professional science academic. This *instrumentalism of the role of science and technology* is deeply engrained in the minds of the Korean science community. The conflict between this utilitarian view of the project-oriented scientists and the pure academic scientists' view was once the source of severe confrontation, but in retrospect, the conflict was the source of energy for a balanced growth in this sector that became indispensable. As the economy is becoming one of the leaders in the world, we are finding that we need a far greater pure-science base than we now have in order to challenge the problems that touch the frontiers of science.

Mr. Jang Mu Lee was the Chairman of the National Science-Technology Supervisory Commission in the same retiring administration. According to him we are in the

---

[56] At the moment a new administration of President Suk Yeol Yoon is running the country.

transition point from fast follower to global frontrunner, and accordingly our research should be network-oriented covering the *resources of the entire world.* With this he demanded Vision, Goals and Blueprints for science research. For this purpose, Korea set up an institute called KISTI (Korea Institute of Science and Technology Information), one of the first in the world. Our science community became ambitious. Some of our public research institutes, such as ETRI, the Electronics Technology Research Institute located in Daejon, Korea, received the world's third highest number of patents granted in competition against major corporations of the world.

South Korea is one of the global leaders in information and communication technologies, and is second only to Germany in Bloomberg's 2020 Innovation Index according to the report by Mark Zastrow, published in *Nature.*[57] Public funding through the National Research Foundation (NRF) rose to 2.5 trillion won (US$2 billion) for basic science research. And roughly equal amount R&D funding is raised by the private sector giant corporations, and this

---

[57] By Mark Zastrow *Nature* | Vol 581 | 28 May 2020, but according to Bloomberg report of 2021, Korea tops the world in its Innovation Index.

funding goes to either their internal research institutes or as grants to university laboratories. Korea now spends 4.5% of its GDP as research money at various levels of research, which is second highest in the world after Israel with 4.9%.[58] According to the IMD of Lausanne University, Swiss in the ratio of R&D investment over GDP, Korea tops the world, and in number of R&D manpower over 1000 population the number one is Korea. In terms of number of articles published in internationally accredited journals Korea stands at 9th in the world.

Research on basic science is gaining attentions and money. Private and public funding sources share roughly equal amount every year. This is the reason for the sudden rise in grants to university labs by private corporations both in and outside Korea. POSTEC is a science and technology university established by POSCO, one of the best steel makers in the world. POSTECH, Pohang University of Science and Technology was founded in 1986 has quickly risen to become one of the world's most innovative uni-

---

[58] Total R&D budgets (in 2018) are US$16.3 billion for Israel, $95.4 billion for Korea, $526 billion for China, and $551.5 billion for the United States. SOURCES: NATURE INDEX; OECD GROSS DOMESTIC SPENDING ON R&D As the Korean GDP in 2018 was around 1.725 trillion dollars, $95.4 billion is 5.53 % instead of 4.5%. *Nature* might have been a little too generous on our GDP.

versities. Reuter's Innovative University Rankings (2019), ranked it the 12th in the world, ahead of the University of California, Johns Hopkins University and Caltech.[59]

## The Korean Research Farm

Sometime in the 1980s, Alvin Toffler said that Seoul has world's highest number of PhDs per capita. Our top-heavy educational demography and obsession with education extended to the highest degree awarded in every discipline. If a young university graduate didn't get a satisfying job at a well-paying major corporation, he went to the graduate school for a higher degree. If a young woman after university graduation didn't get either a satisfying job or a marriage partner, she went to graduate school for further education. There are near two hundred universities in Korea, and the professorial faculties typically obtained

---

[59] Only two universities in the world own the two accelerators owned by POSTECH. The first is the synchrotron radiation accelerator, a third-generation accelerator called the Pohang Light Source-II (PLS-II), and a fourth-generation accelerator, called the Pohang Accelerator Laboratory X-ray Free Electron Laser (PAL-XFEL). Opened to users in 2017, PAL-XFEL, the latter, is the world's most stable XFEL in terms of beam position and energy. PAL-XFEL is indispensable in understanding the phenomena of photosynthesis and chemical reactions in incredibly short time-scales.

their education and degrees from top 50 major American universities or major state universities. The educational qualities of most of Korean universities has dramatically improved as the corporate human resources recruiters' expectations soared high because they can recruit from all over the world. KAIST (Korea Advanced Institute of Science and Technology) is an advanced teaching institution that was established during the early 1970s and its quality of education has risen so quickly that 30% of the new PhD recruits of Samsung Electronics Company usually are new graduates of KAIST after having successfully competed against the PhD graduates of MIT, Cal Tech and other major universities.

According to the latest count, the total number of public research institutes funded by the government is 26. Thirteen of them are listed in the footnote.[60] They recruit post-doctoral level research candidates jointly by the hun-

---

[60] KIST; Korea Institute of Science and Technology
KBSI; Korea Basic Science institute
KASI; Korea Aero-Space Institute
KLSI; Korea Life Science Institute
KSTII; Korea Science-Technology Information Institute
KMRI; Korea Institute for Oriental Medicine
KPTI; Korea Production Technology Institute
Electronic Technology Research Institute

dreds every year. The average salary announced is 97 million won which is close to 90,000 US dollars per year. There are eight provinces and eight autonomous cities directly funded bypassing the provincial governments. All of them are either running their own science research institutes or planning for one. Among them, UIST of Ulsan, and GIST of Gwangju are active in world class research.

One Korean publishing company published the list of all the domestic research centers of private companies that took residence in the nationally organized research farms at four main locations; the cities of Gwangju, Daegu, Daejon, and Busan. The publication lists total 2,459 research teams working in the farms, 219 cases in Gwangju, 340 in Daegu, 1,751 in Daejon, and 149 in Busan. The number of intra-mural research centers of supplier companies to major final product assemblers such as Samsung and Hyundai is countless. Without active and successful research results,

KICT; Korea Institute of Construction Technology
KRISS; Korea Research Institute for Science Standard
KETI; Korea Energy Technology Institute
KERI; Korea Electricity Research Institute
KIMS; Korea Institute of Material Science
Furthermore, there are fourteen other research institutes covering research on national security, green technology, rail technology, chemical research, astrology, safety research and assessment, food technology, nuclear energy, material science and kimchee.

they cannot maintain their supplier status and long term contracts.

In this way the whole country has become a sort of furnace for research and improvement. Literally thousands of companies can assemble color TVs but consumers want something different every year. Mobile phones are the same communication device but consumers want something different and we have to create multi-foldable phones without changing the basic functions of the phone. Consumer addiction to *changes* is so intense, and producers have to change designs to attract consumers. Even the fried-chicken vender running a street corner cart has to change the taste of his products to remain in business. The proprietary chicken taste made by Colonel Sanders is hard to find in Korea and in its place millions of new tastes compete.

Nobel Laureate Economist Robert Lucas published his lecture on 'Making a Miracle' that tries to mathematically theorize the Korean economic miracle. It was published in the journal *Econometrica in March 1993*, the journal of the American Econometric Association. I must commiserate with him for his hardship in this endeavor, for mathematics deny miracles and a miracle is a miracle for it is not rational. Professor Lucas and I share important common ground, however. We both try to offer explanations for the Korean miracle and dismantle the underlying mythology that something mythical had happened. The miraculous history happened as fact, and it was an outcome of a combination of wise strategies, hard work, and amazing timing of events. If the professor can invent an elegant equation like the energy-mass equation of Einstein for the successful economic development that can be transplanted into other countries, we are all prepared to admire him for his genius.

He correctly concludes that the difference in growth trajectory between Korea and Philippines arises from the different *learning curves* of the two communities. His mathematical model stops there and we all accept that conclusion. But this book picks up from there and explains the way superior Korean learning curve derives itself from the changing process of social status of the serfs and poor tenants to middle class, from the way the common goal of erasing poverty naturally passed through each generation, and from the way the obsession for education seamlessly transformed into community-wide competitive research for new technologies that challenged the best in the world. Education is a small part of learning but it is the best part to begin.

If a Paleolithic man visited the Earth now, he would find that modern men live with magic wands for all sorts of purposes. But he would find it hard to understand that such wands are used by everybody, both rich and poor. The critical fact is some of us know how to make the wands and some of us know only how to use them. Clearly science and technology in our world is not a public good that is shared by everybody free of charge. And it is not for sale until it is almost useless. The lesson is clear. Get it, if you are serious about national development.

# IX. The Cancer of Korean Economy

## The Good China, Taiwan

Taiwan is a China. There are two countries in the world who call themselves China; The People's Republic of China, which is the mainland China and the Republic of China, which is Taiwan. Taiwan's territory is about 1/100th as large as mainland China, but before President Nixon and Henry Kissinger traveled to China secretly in 1973 and drove a wedge between China and the Soviet Union, which we call the Nixon Doctrine in action, Taiwan was a permanent member of the UN Security Council with full veto power. The big China in the mainland replaced the small China in Taiwan at every international sphere and took over the membership of international organizations, and international banks. It also took over expensive real estate that Taiwanese embassies occupied all over the world paying zero compensation. The sense of betrayal to the long-time allies from the WWII days must have been heart-breaking to the Taiwanese, and especially so to South Korea.[61]

There was one thing mainland China was not able to replace. Taiwan is a constructive and law-abiding member of the free-world. It was easy for Taiwan to become the *good China*, for the Bad China never stopped behaving internationally in ways that are blatantly against the unwritten rules of the civilized world. China did not hesitate to violate the most common values of humanity in the name of pursuing its national interest. Taiwan was and still is a victim of mainland Chinese brazenness that takes advantage of the slow decision-making process of democracy. To the eyes of communists this democratic tardiness apparently looks like a sign of weakness of the free world.

It is impossible to overly commend the resoluteness of Taiwanese people and its leaders in defending their terri-

---

[61] There is an organization in Korea called Seoul International Forum, where I am a member. We hold annual bilateral meetings with Taiwanese community leaders alternatively in Seoul and Taipei. The scolding we received from the Taiwanese delegates in the meeting right after the break can never be forgotten, especially so because we knew that we betrayed them. Since then we gladly served as the second, but practically only channel of communication between two governments.

tory and continuing to run a free democracy when all odds are against them. When the four Asian dragons started to rise in the early 1980s, Taiwan was one of them. The two city states showed early fatigue due to their limited supply capacity of labor and plant sites. To Korea, Taiwan was the only effective rival in attracting industrial migration and it was almost always one step ahead of Korea in GDP per capita, consumer price stabilization, export surplus and dollar reserve statistics. To this author, who was a young academic economist then, Taiwan was our role model. The Korean industrialization process led by giant corporations called, Jaebol proved to be the only viable strategy, but Taiwan's strategy that was led by small and medium industries was far more popular among academics and economist of financial institutions at the beginning.

But this ranking is completely reversed now. In GDP growth rates, international rankings of national competitiveness, international patents granted, trade surplus, and economic stability, Korea is ahead of Taiwan. This reversal is not well known to the world, but it is important because of the difference in their growth strategies Korea and Taiwan took. This difference reveals a valuable lesson for development planners to pay attention to. I will highlight this point now.

## Does Korean Development Model Need Jaebol?

To most of young Korean economists with degrees earned from American and British universities, Korean economic growth strategy exposed several traps that can kill, we believed, the dynamic growth energy of the Korean economy.

The first was easy growth under government that is too strong. We inherited this excessive governing from the days of military rule at the beginning of the take-off. Industries and markets were too weak to achieve self-correcting market equilibrium. A supply shortage of any article routinely failed to increase supply. In healthy mature market economy, higher market price invites more supply. But in weaker markets, rise of market price is taken as signal to buy up a good before it rises more, rather than to supply more. Higher price only increases demand, instead of reducing it. That's a perversion. Excessive meddling by bureaucrats with market prices caused merchants to lobby the government for price hikes. It provided rich ground for widespread corruption. We saw how the national campaign to build a domestic HMPE industry with the ultimate goal of establishing an independent national defense entailed wide-spread over investment and eventually led to an economic crisis. We paid a huge cost to learn the importance of building a dynamic market that knows how to say no to the government. Economic growth seemed to intensify the symbiotic relationships between business owners and the bureaucrats.

Second, economists were unhappy that Korean corporate owners enjoyed the dividends from chronic developmental inflation. Inflation favored the corporate borrowers, and hurt lenders, the banks and depositors. If there is a 10% inflation rate, companies were given a 10% discount on their liability and bank assets and deposit values are cut by 10% in real values. This encouraged excess corporate borrowing, and it was legitimatized as more borrowing and investment ends up with more production and exports, hence growth. More exports conveniently drew more reinforcements in more governmental nonmonetary subsidies.

Chronic inflation for a developing country is sweet opium that chronically undervalues the exchange ratio and promotes exports.[62] But this opium entails chronic balance of payment deficits by raising the import prices of raw and intermediate materials that a growing country has to import in massive growing quantities.

To the eyes of academic economists, the third and greatest sin was the trend of growing inequity in the distribution of the fruits of economic growth. Economic growth has to be achieved in a way that does not deteriorate the GINI coefficient.[63] Actually our Gini coefficient at 0.345 did not deteriorate as much as in South and Central American countries but that was not the issue to Korean academics. Concentration of wealth and power in the Jaebol corporations was unacceptable to the academics and labor union who never expected Korean corporations could grow into organizations with global stature.

---

[62] If Japan exports a good at one dollar and the yen-dollar exchange ratio is 110 yen per dollar, whereas the true underlying value of yen is 100 yen per dollar, then the exporter gets 10 yen more in revenue by refusing to appreciate yen value to 100 yen per dollar. That is the reason for keeping yen undervalued.

[63] A coefficient of zero would describe a population in which every person receives the same adjusted household income. In contrast, a coefficient of 1 describes the case of maximum income inequality, where one person receives all the income and the rest received none.

In a communitarian country where most of the citizens believe that they are majority shareholders of the society with equal holdings, sharing the poverty was tolerable. But wealth cannot be shared in equal proportion as we grew to be a rich country. If economic growth is bound to make only a few super rich, we worried that this may fundamentally destroy the national communitarian mind set and end the rapid growth of our economy.[64] The middle class of the society can always turn to prefer equity over growth.

By the time the first oil crisis hit the world in 1973, Korea had just finished implementing the second five year economic plan successfully that entailed a major population movement to urban industrial centers. Urban ghettos of constantly mobile workforces sprang up in many large cities, with all the sad stories of the capitalist exploitation of labor typical in early labor-intensive industrial societies producing garments, and textiles. Korean poets, fiction writers, social critics, union agitators, progressive political parties and academics joined in the chorus of resistance

---

[64] Deng Shao Ping declared in his famous speech tour of the Southern Provinces early 1982 "introducing market economy in China will not make all the Chinese rich, and Chines people should be ready for a society where some become rich." China accepted his proposal and 1/3 of China's population still live with income less than 6 dollars a day.

against the strong-handed growth-minded and pro-Jaebol government of Park, Chung Hee, who was assassinated in November 27 of 1978.

At the center of this anger, hatred, and jealousy there were the famous Korean Jaebols as the prime targets and perpetrators. Although insignificant in size compared to the international giants, they were elephants in the small pond of the Korean economy. In the period of the third economic plan of the early 70s and till the early 80s, Korean conglomerates had to create bridgeheads on the totally unknown shores of shipbuilding, consumer electronics, petrochemicals, integrated steel mills, power plants, mechanics and machine building, precision electro-mechanics, construction of major high rises, world class infrastructure, and plant engineering. The Korean elephants had to grow even bigger and the huge international markets permitted them to grow endlessly. However, the minds of domestic critics did not grow, and they had great difficulty in accepting the big corporations growing even bigger while 'people' remained just wage earners.

Business leaders, positively charged with self-confidence after the two successful economic planning experiences, entertained very different dreams that could be summarized as 'What the Japanese do, we can do better.' Mr. Jung, Ju Young, the successful founder of Hyundai Construction Company, origin of the Hyundai Motors Group, is reported to have said, "In both the construction of buildings and ships we erect the steel frame first, then for buildings you cloth them with glass, and for ships you cloth them by welding steel plates and adding the engines bought from an engine company." This is the reason that he started to build ships, even though he had zero previous experience.

The cold reality is that economies of scale were of critical importance in these industries, and for sheer survival in the international market, Korean Jaebol had to plan their investments in a scale as big as, or even bigger than their Japanese and European counterparts. Government assistance inevitably and significantly grew compared to the 60s that focused on textiles and light industries. The international comparative advantage of Korean companies in HMPE industries was, frankly, miserable. Some form of substantial size of government assistance was necessary because Jaebol entered into the HMPE and weapons industries due to the *strong guidance* of the government.

Planning the international scale in each industry is understandable but question rises where did they get the idea of building a full set economy in Korea, one that produces everything from tissue paper, cement and tiles to semiconductors, LNG carriers and jet fighters? President Park and his close associates never believed that the US armed forces would stay on the Korean Peninsula forever and we should prepare for the eventual independent self-defense. That is a good reason for building a full range of mechanical, electronic, heavy and petrochemical industries. But academics had worries about this. To them the never ending expansion of business area by Jaebol was nothing other than manifestation of endless greed, and they labeled their strategy as the octopus-style grabbing to justify more land, loans from banks and government subsidies.

Academic economists, including this author, publicly declared that the *Jaebol problem* is the cancer of the Korean economy that will one day require a major medical operation. The animosity was so intense that lowering interest rates during downturns of cycle was vehemently opposed by academics, for Jaebol were the largest borrowers and hence the biggest beneficiaries of low interest.[65] The fact that a lower interest rate promotes more investment and economic growth didn't matter to them. They believed that the fruits of growth were monopolized by the Jaebol.

While Korean companies were struggling in an uphill battle in HMPE industries, our clever neighbor Taiwan was enjoying sustained and stable growth with exports of bicycles and tennis rackets where they became number one in the world. That gave an added boost to the criticism by the academic sector. Jaebol were regarded as the cause of all the Korean economic sins including a military industrial conspiracy. This anti-corporate sentiment in the Korean academia during the 70's was inherited by the so called *386 generation*, the Korean indigenous socialist politicians, who succeeded in electing three presidents with progressive socialist ideology.

---

[65] When I joined Samsung by the personal invitation of the founder, one US embassy councilor in charge of commerce told me that he believed I was a spy from the public sector sent to a Jaebol. Even foreigners thought Jaebol were not part of Korea. I accepted the invitation because after twenty years of studying, researching and teaching economics, I found that I knew very little about how the real economy worked. The invitation gave me the opportunity to learn about and see the economy in action right from the center. After forty years, I am still learning.

# Small and Medium Industry of Taiwan

There are a vast number of research reports on the role of small and medium enterprises in Taiwan's economic development. The majority view on this question is positive. Taiwan SMEs contributed up to 70% of the total exports of Taiwan during the period of the 60s to the 80s according to the Taiwan SME White Papers.[66] SMEs provided more than 80% of the total employment of Taiwan, but provided less than half of the total production. The positive role of SMEs in the economic development and industrialization of Taiwan seems unquestionable. This bias in favor of SMEs in Taiwan is extraordinary compared to other industrial countries.

To the Korean academic economist, the developmental strategy of Taiwan looked like an ideal combination of fast growth, stability, export competitiveness, and employment generation, with fairer income distribution.[67] But the other side of the same picture is that the labor productivity of

---

[66] 'White Paper on Taiwan's SME 1991 p.288 Small and Medium Enterprise Administration, Ministry of Economic Affairs, Taipei, Taiwan.

[67] Actually income distribution of Korea was not worse than Taiwan according to the World Bank statistics. Gini coefficient of Taiwan and Korea were 31.6 and 33.9 in 2012 and remained largely stable since then.

Taiwan has to be lower in average compared to countries where a large number of giant corporations are operating with modern plants and equipment. Substantial research money and time was spent around the world to determine whether this SME-led growth strategy is a textbook model for the aspiring development economists. Korea is now offering evidence that an SME-biased strategy may not be the correct one.[68]

While economists did not reach an agreement on the superiority of this Taiwan strategy, the Korean experience, which is not quite a well-designed strategy but more like an unexpected outcome, seem to provide a valid answer to this question. If you want to become a member of leading group of *industrializing* countries with robust growth rate, stable economy, fair distribution, good employment rates, the Taiwan solution seems to be the right answer. But if you refuse to remain an industrializing country, and wish to

---

[68] 'A Comparison of the Performance of SMEs in Korea and Taiwan: Policy Implications for Turbulent Times by C. Hall Macquarie Graduate School of Management and Charles Harvie University of Wollongong,(charvie@uow.edu.au) University of Wollongong Research Online Faculty of Business-Economics Working Papers, Faculty of Business and Law January 2003
'Taiwan's Economic Development: The Role of Small and Medium-sized Enterprises beyond the Statistics' Marco Veselka, a paper presented at the Second Conference of the European Association of Taiwan Studies, Ruhr University Bochum, 1 - 2 April 2005.

proceed to becoming one of the *post-industrial countries*, where only those with cutting edge science and technology compete, Taiwan's strategy clearly is not the right one. Korea is entering into this world.

The high-tech industries, internet and telecommunications, artificial intelligence, semiconductors, and opportunities that the new metaverses create cannot be *planned* to take roots in one's territory. China's IC chips industry is one good example of failed plans to transplant the semiconductor industry into China with billions of dollars of government money to aid private and public semiconductor companies. Private companies practically stole the grants in money, and disappeared over night. Public companies like Tsing Hwa University Group, while remaining relatively honest in dispensing the grant money, gave up the attempt to transplant advanced semiconductor industry into China.[69] The China-decoupling policy of President Trump that Mr. Biden inherited with more intensity blocked the pipelines of semiconductor technology and critical facility supplies.

---

[69] Our experience reveals that the success in the semiconductor industry is far from guaranteed just by securing the fabricating technology. The yield rates per silicon wafer rises by the dedicated workers on the worksites who submitted on average over 100 daily suggestions to improve the production processes to raise the yield rates. In other words, workers became researchers.

The aggressively hostile territorial policies of the Communist Party of China (CCP) on international waters, or on the border lands shared with neighbors, and the repeated trade retaliation against policies of neighboring governments collectively made recruiting scientists from Korea and Japan impossible. In today's intellectual-property protection culture stealing brains with high compensation is very difficult to succeed.

If you are not already in a high-tech industry as one of the strong competitors, you better restrain yourself from wasting money in this dangerous terrain. If you are one step ahead of your competitors, such as possessing the ability to fabricate 12 inch silicon wafers in fine circuitry of 4 nano meter width with an 80% yield rate, you normally block the path behind you that you just experienced in your research for improved chip designs. Your rivals have to go through the same situation where you discovered your unique solution. By patenting all the techniques and knowhow that will be critical for them in getting close to where you are, you make your rivals task several times harder than your experience. That means your rivals will never get to where you are today or if they do, they will have to invent new ways to circumvent the road you monopolize. That is why the speed of the technological improvement of number one is faster than number two, and the gap never stops increasing. Every day in the high tech industry there is a Chicken Game. It is a brutal world.[70] Only the best survives. The probability of success in the SME type industries is much higher than HMPE industries and high-tech industries.

## Metastasis of the Korean Economic Cancer

Market capitalization value of Samsung group companies is about twenty percent of the entire Korean stock market value. The same of the 20 largest Jaebol groups in Korea share about half of Korean total market capitalization value. Statistics are not available but sum of company values of the dedicated supplier chains of these conglomerates should be equal or close to the value of the mother company, namely Jaebols. The Korean cancer is spreading

---

[70] Japan decided to attack Pearl Harbor because the USA blocked the route of oil imports according to Japanese. If semiconductor is as important as oil to China, as one modern car typically needs 3000 chips per car, one wonders whether Chinese leaders would launch their hyper-sonic Dung Fung missiles to Guam or Hawaii in order to capture Taiwan and TSMC technology. One American academic even suggested destroying TSMC Taiwan plants to fend off Chinese missiles.

in spite of all sorts of government restriction and would soon reach 80% of the market value. Metastasis of Korean cancer may eventually conquer the nation unless they find their economic territory outside Korea.

Direct employments of the mother companies and the indirect employments by supplier clusters of Sobujang (materials, components and facilities) frequently create a city or two where shops, markets, schools, beauty shops, restaurants, hospitals, public offices jointly create the *cluster effect* at vicinity. Samsung used to run a semiconductor plant at a city in central China called Hui Jou near river Yang Tze. When high wages of China forced Samsung to shut down the plant and left, after paying all the early retirement benefits, the city turned into an instant ghost town overnight. The cancer cell has been cut off.

Korean national assembly passed a law that prohibits monetary donation from corporate funds to political parties. It will be very hard for politicians to resist the temptation to extort money from the giant Korean corporations who are politically powerless. Actually covert extortions do take place, for occasionally corporate leaders are indicted and sentenced for bribing. If President Joe Biden arrested Jeff Bezos and have him indicted for donating money to the American Olympic Society, people will lough. But that is possible in Korea.[71] Nobody knows better than the communists how to manipulate the democratic system, the media and the public that sometimes turn foolish and mad, hitting the street by half a million deluded by false reports.

Conveniently members of the previous administrations are always the target for trial over bribery. Since the tenure of administration is 5 years only, without right to run for the second term, we perfected a system of discrete cancer surgery every five years, and the Jaebol leaders became convenient scape goats. Even the socialist politicians now admit that the great Korean corporations are the truly valuable national resources, without that Korea cannot compete in the global markets. But Korean people are alarmed and

---

[71] Jae Yong Lee is the grandchild of the founder of Samsung Group and until recently was the CEO, vice chairman of Samsung Electronics Co. before he was sentenced to serve a jail term for the money he donated to the Korean Equestrian Society, that the court declared an indirect bribery. Court declared that this sports group is an "Economic Common Body" with the now jailed former president Keun Hye Park; a unique interpretation never heard in the history of jurisprudence. For reader's information, everybody in Korea, including the courts, knows that former president Park did not receive a single penny from Mr. Lee. This will be recorded as a wart in the history of Korean Judiciary.

proud as well by their amazing technological progress that knows no boundary.

Without these cancerous Jaebol group of companies, Korean economy would be weaker than Philippines in agricultural outputs, weaker than Algeria in mining, and weaker than Thailand in service industries. In the 1950s after the Korean war, Korean manufacturing sector for all practical purpose did not exist except textiles for school uniforms, handmade shoes, coal mining and briquettes. Now Korean Jaebol can design and make unmanned nuclear-powered submarines equipped with SLBM (submarine-launched ballistic missiles) that can be fired deep under the ocean completely undetected. It takes a globally organized Jaebol corporation to source, manufacture, market and deliver even such common household products as Na Myon, or Mandoo, half-cooked frozen Korean instant foods, because only those companies with global organization of thousand reliable agencies and distributors can guarantee the delicate hygienic standards. They have far more to lose when caught in non-compliance and deception.

# Big Is Beautiful

In 1998, I had my short article published on the Singapore weekly magazine Far Eastern Economic Review with the title, 'Big Is Beautiful.'[72] The title was editor's choice which I thought commercialized too much. This was the period when 'Small is Beautiful' culture of Japan was trendy and Taiwanese economic growth strategy based on SME was regarded as the text book model for economic development. Korean economy that over-invested in heavy mechanical and petro-chemical industries rammed into a major economic crisis of corporate shut downs and massive bank failures. Korea was regarded as the bad boy in the economic development class. But this Korean weakness turned into the Korean strength.

The editor asked me to explain why Samsung Group safely weathered the crisis while Daewoo did not. With all the resources and opportunities available to the big Jaebols, I wondered why should one go bankrupt. Firstly we had

---

[72] 'Big Is Beautiful-Debunking the Myth of Small Business' is a book title published by MIT press, coauthored by Robert D. Atkinson and Michael Lind. The book demonstrates why small business is not the basis of American prosperity, not the foundation of American democracy, and not the champion of job creation. Apparently America is not Taiwan.

the global network of offices in 120 cities of 64 countries. That is a vast organization sending enormous amount of business information very few in the world know that they exist. Some of our executives stayed in a same city for over 20 years building effective human networks of individuals mutually exchanging business information. At least two of my former subordinates who spoke local languages fluently married local girls to settle in those countries. Both became Muslims. I was truly impressed by their goal-oriented life style with intense dedication.

Large corporations usually maintain huge data base. Expert groups screen and evaluate the opportunities and risks of major proposals and prioritize the fund allocations for both now and future. Some funding is for ordering large quantity of para-xylene or nickel before the price rises steeply. Some funding is for buying up the stock of a company who possesses a monopoly technology useful for our semiconductor fabrication or LNG carriers. Our decision has to be in the highest quality that any corporation should make. Only our big size enabled it.

In developing countries the most serious bottle neck for

business is access to fund, and Korean Jaebols solved this problem by *cross ownership* of any new project. Company A, B, and C were mutually cross-owned from the beginning, and typically called to invest in the shares of new company D. Now if company A started a new project of vital importance, then all the member companies of the group are called for cash injection to this project including company D. There is no holding company but the cross ownership works better for keeping the system safe. We had to defend from hostile takeover of our companies that is traditionally paying out low dividends by complicated cross ownership structure. Korea was so intensely growth-oriented that dividends were charged with high taxes. That came back with Korea-discount in stock prices but sent wolves away.

As time passes and the number of group companies reach over 60 to 200, and the ownership will be thinly spread, but the tradition of assisting investment each other between member companies continued, as some sort of insurance for rainy days. When one of the 60 companies falls into a trouble, all the 59 companies come to help to prevent an epidemic. It is very dangerous for the reverse can happen too. This corporate safety net helps when most of the member companies are making healthy profits. When many of them make losses or one of them makes serious loss, then the whole system can go wrong. Daewoo was one such victim.

Advanced research is only a part of the technology race. We needed a systematic organization of suppliers, to whom we can disclose our advanced research projects several years before we disclose to the world what we will put on the market soon. Samsung Electronics Co. has three layers of supplier network. Samsung Display Industry (SDI), Samsung Data System (SDS), and Samsung Electric Devices (SED) are member companies of the group hence make the first layer. The second layer is consisted of about 200 suppliers who made long term contract with the mother company, hence are the privy to the confidential technical plans for the products to be put on the market several years ahead. Without their successful development of new component and parts, Mother Company cannot create the new product promised to the market.

The third layer suppliers is consisted of over 2000 and they are mostly suppliers to the second layer suppliers. Even such simple device as remote controller of TV set requires plastic case maker, mold maker for the case, semiconductor and foundry, LCD display maker. Healthy business relation of these small companies with the mother company, and the quality of their products determines the success and failure of new products in the market. Creating future supply system is equivalent to managing a system of research units, big or small, all aiming one identical goal of putting the best product in the world ahead of competitors.

When you are big enough to supply more than 50% of the entire global market, you have the privilege to optimize the supply logistics of parts and components and final products, as well as optimizing the location of production and logistic sites best to serve the market you aim at. When a mother company moves, whether it is from China to Vietnam, Hungary, Czech, or Slovakia, hundreds of supplier companies follow. When that happens, the local economy jumps up by a chain reaction. Production facilities are sunken costs and to save capital costs, companies continue to use them until they are really outdated. But when assembly plant of the mother company moves internationally, old equipment and facilities of the suppliers are also discarded.

Production facilities are frequently modernized and automated with the latest available machines whenever there is a big move from a country. This fact alone can make the competition unfair. Cost of removal is more than compensated by this improvement in productivity.

Finally the scale of marketing expense of big companies is a dream to the small competitors. This spring Samsung Electronics Co. bought up simultaneously the entire 20 advertisement spaces available at the Times Square, and filled all the boards with Samsung advertisement. Like Apple, big companies try to construct a whole new eco-system that may assure a long term mutual dependence between the company and the consumers. Big companies dream different dreams.

## Fate or Strategy

In retrospect, it is clear that Korean economy would not have arrived where it is now, if it were not for the brilliant success of our Jaebols and their advanced high-tech industries. But Korean conglomerates appeared and grew not naturally by the market. It was a result of deliberate and rational responses to the rapidly changing global economy. The first and most painful event was the *ending of American economic aids* in late 1950s. Entire world depended on the American economic aids. America opened its domestic market for free access to the former aid receivers of Marshall Plan. Korea created *the corporations*, future Jaebols, to export unknown products to this unknown market. East-Asian countries including Korea started to play the role that China plays now in much smaller scales. From the genesis Korean economic growth came from exports of manufactured goods, and it was not a mission suitable to street-shop SMEs.

After 10 years of light industrial exports by Korea, the OPEC cartel was born and hit the world economy with stagflation. I explained before in this new opportunities and new rules of game prevailed in the HMPE and construction industries. Big-scale orders came from *nouveau riche* of oil-rich countries who chose lowest bidding price of the Korean bidders with no experiences. Without this shocking change under global oil crisis, Korean industries would have been shut off from the market that always demands success records for pre-qualification screening, which we didn't have. Korean companies were neither competitive in costs nor in qualities. All we had was *our speed* which we turned into *profit margins*. With the help of oil money, we changed the rules in these industries of HMPE and constructions. Korean Jaebols became globally competitive companies.

Democratic Party of USA was not very happy with the huge spending of federal budget by the US ground forces stationed in Korea. All the Ford-Carter-Reagan administrations almost withdrew GIs from Korea. It did not happen, but left a lasting impact in Korea's economic policy, ie. new focus on the building up a *defense industry*; both development technology and mass-production capability. Korean Jaebols had to go through a managerial nightmare, for unlike other heavy machines, chemicals, ships, and cars, products of defense industry cannot be exported. Quality was bad for we didn't have the technology. And if the technology is obtained by contract, the contract bans exporting. However by the order of strong government, and partly for patriotism, Jaebols invested heavily in these new ventures, and it required huge capital commitments. Korean military did not like their products either and it became later another cause for the massive write-offs.

Eighties was chaotic period under extended military rule with endless street demonstrations by students. For Jaebols a critical turning point arrived and Jaebols got a chance to resolve their managerial problems by technological development. In less than ten years from the announcement of Korean independent defense industry, a totally unexpected source of defense industry technology appeared by the collapse of Soviet Union. At the peak of Russian moratorium under President Boris Yeltsin, Korea lent over 1.3 billion dollars in hard currency to help the new Russian government with whom we just opened a formal diplomatic relationship. Russia wanted to pay back the debt in goods. The result was significant transfer of *hard and soft wares of Russian military industry*. Unlike the American technology, Russians did not ban our exports of defense industry products that partly used Russian technology or components.

Interestingly this was the same period when Samsung decided to challenge the semiconductor memory industry and it coincides with appearance of personal computers and related operational software industry in the market. But most importantly this is the period when US government decided to release its world-wide web of internet services. Unfortunately for Japan this is the period when it started to fall into the lost 30 years of recession or stagnation.

Jaebols and the entire Korean manufacturing industries were in some sort of limbo. Export composition of Korea is now occupied mostly by HMPE products of low quality and price. Light industrial products exports became unimportant as the engine of growth. Hyundai Motors exported small sedans called Pony but frequently they were objects of jokes and ridicules. Korea exported household electronics goods such as low quality color TVs but the US government slapped heavy anti-dumping tariffs as Korea did not broadcast TV programs in color yet, to avoid rapid rise in electricity consumption. Nearly all the Jaebols were bleeding in the investment on weapons industry.

## None but the Best Deserves to Survive

Seventies were the period of birth for Korean HMPE

industries, and eighties were period for survival for them. Miraculous birth of Korean HMPE industries with fanfare did not guarantee survival of them and eighties was the test period of their survival. In light industries such as textiles and shoes, there are always markets for second and third rate products and your shabby goods with low price survived. In the sophisticated market of machines, electronics, and chemicals markets for second and third rate products did not exist and if they did that was for a short time where one has to dump the unsold products before liquidation. We did not know that the high quality in this industry comes from advanced technology not from dedications and skills of workers or cheap wages. Under this circumstance Samsung started its semiconductor venture.

Reverse engineering the advanced Russian weapons gave many solutions to the weapon makers who met technological dead ends all around. But to other HMPE makers it was only a partial help. They needed an entirely *new strategy* to transform the third rate Korean HMPE makers into a first rate producers of highest quality products that all the rich consumers of the world love. K.H. Lee is a son of B.C Lee the founder of Samsung who inherited the responsibility of managing the group. One of the first things he did after inauguration was to stage a drama of dumping all the low quality electronic and electric goods of Samsung on the ground and put them to fire to dramatize the departure from the days of third rate producer, and mark the end of his father's days. The entire group started a campaign for producing best quality products or stop production. No cost was spared if it was to reach the global best in quality. If any one of the company failed this task, it was taken as a signal for closure of the company. 'Either the best or drop out' was the rule.

Mong Gu Chung, is the heir of Hyundai Motor group and his strategy for transformation of his group was no less dramatic. One morning out of nowhere, he announced a new corporate policy of ten(10) year guarantee and ten-year free service for all the vehicles the company exported. The global standard product guarantee used to last only 3 years and 30,000 miles in the early 1990s. This was his way for issuing a directive that said 'Make cars that are free of trouble for ten years and if you fail, let's close down the plants for we have no future'. If we continue making cars just as good as our competitors', we will be squeezed out, and we don't have any future for it is not our market. Mercedes, BMW, and Toyota own the markets. Equal level of quality and performance is the short cut for suicide. We will be driven out of it eventually. We needed a shock but this time *we had to make* the shock.

When China joined the WTO and started to hijack all the manufacturing activities like a black hole in early 1990s, we thought Korea was about to be cracked by a nut cracker made of Japan on top and China at bottom. The internal social energy that drove Korean development in the 70s and 80s simply were not enough for our survival in this new circumstance created by the arrival of oversized neighboring competitor. Our engine of growth was about to stop and we actually met one in 1997 crisis. The above two business leaders correctly saw that the only way out of this crisis is to become the best in the world which is loved by the world all over. Industrial powers come and go, and when Korea collapses there will be nobody to sob on our behalf. Only the best is irreplaceable and the world doesn't care for the numerous mediocrities.

When we entered into the unknown world of HMPE

industries in 1970s, we had to target the cheapest product cost and bidding price. When we found our price is not low enough, we reduced our delivery time to reduce costs. And we won the projects and sold our equipment. Now in the early 1990s and through the economic crisis, we had to change our target to disregard the cost and focus on adding new functions and qualities that our competitor products did not have. We offered performance and quality guarantees that the world never saw. We put our hearts and sole into our products and services that astonished our clients. Every January at the CES exhibitions at Las Vegas, we surprised the world with the world's brightest, thinnest, and biggest TV screens that the world did not know whether it wanted or not. They were not for the world; they were for a few super rich who decided who the best is. The majority follows the super-rich and chose our cheaper versions instead of the second best. We found that the higher the price of our leading flagship model, the more we sell in the general markets.

To be fair, it must be pointed out that somebody had to deliver the world's best product for this strategy to work. It was the CEOs of divisions such as mobile phones, semiconductors, household electronics, aerospace, or shipbuilding who had to create the world's best products. When the projects fail, it is their head that fell on the ground, not the engineers, his deputies, or even the group chairman. These division CEOs were selected and groomed for thirty years within the corporate organizations. Less than 20 new CEOs are promoted to this position each year in entire Korean corporate groups. Korea should be thankful to their hard work.

Korean companies had a special privilege that they don't have to keep their stock prices high. Disregarding the company' stock price would cost the head of the CEO in America. But in Korean companies, not only was the dividend tax high, but also the resource for the dividend, the profit, was low too. Toyota Motors is notorious for squeezing dry towels in order to get a drop of water, and the dry towels are the component suppliers. In order to minimize inventory level of Toyota plants, and reduce production costs, supplier trucks were kept outside the Toyota plants waiting on the road for days until they are called into the assembly plants to meet the rule of just-in-time delivery of parts and components. This just-in-time inventory management model of Toyota was taught as text book model at MBA courses without reports of the sacrifices of suppliers. Such practice is impossible in Korea, for the labor union will call reporters and make a headline in next-morning new papers and the CEO will be dismissed. Democracy works in inscrutable ways. Lower profit of the mother company can ensure healthy bottom lines of suppliers and their research capabilities for long term joint product development.

Under such circumstance it was not wise for great Korean corporations to maximize profits for that would intensify pressure for higher supply prices of parts and components, internal wages, or attract high pressures for dividend, or higher taxes. Traditionally Korean corporations competed each other for higher sales and export volumes and technology progress, rather than higher profits. Higher exports, more employments, and tax payments to the government were always rewarded sumptuously by the government in various forms of subsidies, access to scarce capital funding, and import quota for expensive materials. Government permitted all sorts of special-purpose internal capital reservations such as international market development fund, overseas resource development fund, technology development fund, and manpower training fund.

The entire system was focused to increase investment and corporate growth and the national economic growth. But this system opened wide tax evasion opportunities to the owners of corporations, and the government invented a strange tax called *inferred dividend tax* for dividends that did not exist. Nonetheless, the point was that the whole system and country was tuned to be pro-growth, and corporations who danced to this tune grew bigger and richer, medium size supplier companies grew in the same proportion, and the cost of this disregard to the stock-owner interest crystalized in what is known as the Korea Discount in the stock market. This kept the international portfolio investment away from Korean market until the foreign exchange shortage crisis of 1997, which made anything Korean very cheap and accessible.

Most importantly this managerial cushion of internal reserves gave resources for research and development for the highest product quality and some globally new products such as LED displays, Lithium batteries, and

CPU-on-Memory semiconductors. Unlike the American CEOs who has to borrow huge amount of money to buy up their company stocks to keep the stock prices high, and keep their neck safe, Korean CEOs devoted their time and energy in dreaming the next generation products and technology and laying the ground for capturing the market before their competitors.

Mr. Noguchi Yukio is an honorary professor of economics at the Hitotzubashi University and worked at the ministry of finance of Japanese government where he retired. In December 2021 he contributed an article on the Kendai Business magazine where he analyzed the process of Korea-Japan economic reversal during last 30 years. What he explains is basically same as what most other outsiders knew and agreed that Japanese economy remained stagnant during the lost thirty years in spite of the aggressive easy money policy of Prime Minister Shinzo Abe, or perhaps because of it.

Professor Noguchi criticizes that the government and industry leaders of Japan took the easy option of reducing the export prices of their products as China started to export massive quantity of HMPE products in prices no other country can compete. The typical weight of wage cost in the export prices of HMPE products is around 5% and never exceeded 8%. Cheap wage helped but cannot beat the effect of cheap currency which can be devalued by 10 % instantly. Mr. Abe's two arrows, aggressive supply of money and irresponsible expansion of government debt entailed cheap Yen and easy solution to China assault in exports. According to Mr. Noguchi this addiction to cheap Yen turned Japanese economy and industries into chronic patient that need for more morphine incapable of coming to shape by itself.

Korean industries on the other hand discovered that they are about to be squeezed out of the market by the double pressures of cheap China products and high quality Japanese products. Very wisely the Korean industrial leaders understood the brutality of the market that permits only the best to survive in the upper market and the cheapest in the lower market. Consumers do not need anything in between. Since Korea cannot compete against the cheap wages and arbitrary exchange rate policy of China, the only viable option left to us was to challenge the best of the world. If we fail, theoretically we can get back to poverty and start competing against China again. We knew that this option did not exist to us, for it meant communist revolution in Korea instigated by China and North Korea.

To everybody's astonishment semiconductor division of Samsung Electronics announced in the autumn of 1986 that its San Jose center of semiconductor research succeeded, for the *first time in the world*, in designing the one mega dynamic random access memory chips (DRAM). Three years ago, Mr. B.C.Lee, CEO of Samsung group announced that Samsung will put the future of the group in the 'commodity chips' namely the 64K DRAM that is produced in massive quantity in identical units and is subject to the danger of being pushed out of the market instantly as soon as somebody designs next generation chip with 4 times greater capacity of memory compared to existing chips. In just two generations from 64 K and 256K, on August 1, 1986, barely three years after it started producing the dynamic memory chips, Samsung jumped to the top of the world by creating the 1 Mega DRAM first time in the world. Since then, it never gave up the throne for 30 years.[73]

---

[73] History of Korean semiconductor industry goes back to 1962 when Dr. Kidong Kang

Little we knew about this highly risky and volatile industry in the late 1980s. Becoming a member with buyer's accreditation in this extremely hostile semiconductor community is hard enough, but becoming the leader of them requires a miracle. In 2021 entire sum of profits made by 9 top electronics companies of Japan is less than half of Samsung Electronics Company profit. All the dynamic random access memory (DRAM) chips makers of Japan stopped producing them except one, Toshiba Memory, which is planned to close down, whereas Samsung alone supplies more than half of the global market and SK Semiconductor Co, another Korean company and Micron of USA shares the rest.

This DRAM is called the 'commodity semiconductor' which is needed in large quantity by computer and server makers, just as any mature product components or bolt nuts, but unlike mature products only the best with the most

---

received PhD degree in semiconductor technology at the Ohio State University and started his career at Motorola. In 1974 he returned to Korea and established the Korea Semiconductor Co., which was sold to Samsung Electronics Co in 1978. Another stream of Korean semiconductor development was made by ETRI (Korea Electronic Technology Research Institute) that made 64 K ROM (read only memory) in 1982 that is used mainly for consumer electronic goods which requires far less memory capacity than computers.

advanced technology survives, for the computer and server makers would not buy inefficient memory chips with larger power consumption when better chips are available in the market in strategically competitive prices.[74] The new comer has to sell their new products at prices that leave hardly any margins or simply give up. Because the investment size for memory mass production is near ten billion dollars per line,[75] if you fail to make profits in the latest investment with your latest technology, you will have to close down your company. It is a very cruel chicken game that Sharp taught Samsung when the latter joined the DRAM market in the 1980's. That is why when one company succeeds developing new and most efficient DRAM, say from 4 mega DRAM to 16 mega DRAM, then, the rest automatically drops out of the market altogether, unless it has enough internal capital and technological power to beat the leader at the next higher level product.

Korean shipbuilders now take nearly 100% of LNG

---

[74] Like human beings Data travel and stay at hotels called IDC, Internet Data Center but unlike people they consume huge amount of electricity. According to one estimate they consume about 1.5 % of the total power consumption on earth. Semiconductor memory is the main user of this power in server operations and cooling.

[75] The EUV (Extreme Ultra Violet) photo-exposure machine by ASML of Netherland costs about 200 million dollars per unit for 4 nano meter circuitry.

tank carrier orders. This carrier is propelled by power generated in solid oxide fuel cells that use the vaporized LNG. Hyundai Motor Co. leads the world in hydrogen trucks. Daewoo Ship Building Co. built 4000-ton submarine equipped with SLBM and plans to build a nuclear-powered submarine, using SMR (Small Modular Reactor) designed by the Korea Atomic Energy Agency. ADD(Agency for Defense Development) successfully fired SLBM, and plans to send an unknown number of GPS and surveillance satellites in cooperation with US NASA. KF-21 is the name of a semi-stealth jet fighter designed and produced by the Korea Aerospace Industry (KAI), contracted to supply to the air force of Korea and some foreign governments. Hanjin Co. a company under Korean Air Lines Group has developed a stealth naval version of this jet fighter to be carried on a new naval aircraft carrier designed jointly with Babcock of UK and Hyundai Ship Building Corp. K9 mobile artillery that has the highest target-hitting rate among its cohorts is produced by Hanwha Defense Industry. These and lot more are what the Korean Jaebols do now. When one aims for the best in the world, even if one fails reaching the best, such attempt leaves substantial technology by-products that help in the long run.

This benevolent cancer of the Korean economy never stops growing its tumor but Koreans now admit that we cannot enjoy a present level of prosperity without the creative roles of Korean conglomerates. Jaebols became an integral part of what Korea is now. In international relations and technology progress, they are already ahead of the Korean government. Many suspect that Korean socialist governments wanted to nationalize the ownership of Jaebols.

Did Korean economic and social development need Jaebol? The geopolitical character of Korea demanded a strong military and vital defense industry, which in turn demanded a healthy and high-tech HMPE industry and the Korean Jaebols can handle this task. It is obvious that the SME-led Taiwan model cannot do it. If anything, we need more of them with new missions in the new AI industry electric cars, unmanned vehicles and high-tech weapons, green energies, industrial and military robots, service industry robots, unmanned delivery systems, and entertainment in the meta-verse worlds.

As a strategy for other developing countries, the message from the Korean experience is, to be honest, depends on the assessment of your situation. There is no strategy without risks of failure. Some countries have to run fast like Korea did, in spite of fearful risks. If any country can take a gradual approach and minimize the risk of failure, I would consider that a blessing of God.

## Appendix

## Inside the Taiwan Miracle

Every successful economy deserves a claim for a miracle for escaping the poverty that lasted millennia. The vicious circle of poverty demands profound social dislocation that we call a revolution. Surviving such nation-wide shake-ups and coming out as a rich industrial country is so hard that more than two hundred countries in this world failed the mission. Chen Been-lon is a research fellow at the Institute of Economics at Academia Sinica, Taiwan. He wrote an insightful article with this title and reveals strengths and weaknesses of Taiwan's economy.[76]

---

[76] "Inside Taiwan Miracle' by Chen, Been-lon, , available on Wikipedia, June 01,2011 Taipei, Taiwan

According to him, Taiwan's territory is similar in size to that of the Netherlands with a population of just 23 million. He is proud that Taiwan plays a leading role in the international high-tech industry and was ranked as the world's 25th-largest economy in 2009. Economic development accelerated under the Japanese colonial rule (1895–1945). The farm sector continued to grow with tea trade that began under the the Qing dynasty (1683–1895). But farmers added rice and sugar cane farming under Japanese rule. In the latter years of the Japanese era, the manufacturing of fertilizer and textiles led the economic growth. In 1899, ten years before Korea was annexed by Japan, and 52 years before Korea recovered its independence, the colonial government of Japan in Taipei established a 'fundamental pillar of the island's economy by creating a central bank called the Bank of Taiwan.'

In 1945, when World War II ended, 'the Japanese surrendered to the Republic of China (ROC) government in Nanjing, mainland China. In Taiwan, the ROC government took ownership of all former Japanese capital, both public and private. Because Japanese capital had been spread throughout all economic sectors except for rice farming, the extent of ROC ownership was likewise pervasive after the handover,' capital and land holdings alike.

Two points stand out. One; there is undeniable nostalgia for the Japanese rule, and two; the ROC government that came from the the mainland with Kuo Min Tang party is just another foreign ruler that is not any better than the Japanese. In fact, in 1915 student revolt against the Japanese's rule,(called Typhany Incident) more than 800 people were killed, and in the 1930 Uso Incident, 644 were killed on the street and 216 were executed by the Japanese. But in the 1948 student revolt against the Kuo Min Tang government, General Chen is reported to have killed nearly 40,000 Taiwanese youngsters. It could easily be an exaggeration, but if it is, the fact that people want to exaggerate the number carries a greater message.

Shifting the gravity of Taiwan's economy from agriculture to manufacturing was the first task of ROC government and the first step was to assist wide range of import substitution industries. Taiwan started this policy in 1949, one year before the Korean War. It was directly against the classical economic theory but worked very well, because importing any product in large-scale is physical evidence that there exists a great domestic market for that product, and guaranteed sufficient scale of production that helped raising productivity to international standard. Chemical fiber and textile was the industry that Taiwan focused from the first economic plan (1953-56) and by the end of the 1980s, Taiwan became the second largest supplier of chemical fiber and textile products in the world. It started the journey of industrialization 9 years ahead of Korea's first economic plan that started in 1962. Sadly the success in this light industry became a sweet toxin that significantly reduced the need for risk taking in other manufacturing industries that required complicated technologies that Taiwan did not have. SMEs of Taiwan grew to global scale, but their managerial minds remained SME.

Then there came a *solution* to this problem of risk-aversion in the form of OEM production. From 1961 Japanese consumer electronics companies gave consignment production orders of transistor radios on a large scale to Taiwan. This is the beginning of the industrial migration by segmentation of production processes in search of lower-wage countries. The company that received the consignment order did not need to develop modern technology. It was given to them with the OEM order and the segment that was outsourced is usually very labor-intensive without much technology, mostly assembly. As long as the OEM producer meets the quality requirements of the importing company, there is no marketing risk; two birds with one stone.

According to Mr. Akio Morita, then chairman of Sony, of the book *Made in Japan* fame, he received 500,000 order of transistor radio from GE for OEM production with offer to lend the capital needed for plant, and he refused it. This was in early 1950s, less than 10 years after the invention of semiconductors in the Bell Lab of America. Sony was a small startup company in the 1950s and if he took the offer, he envisioned that Sony will never get over the sweet toxin that binds Sony as the eternally dedicated supplier of GE.

A tenacious desire for independence determines the culture of states and corporations. The love of risk-free manufacturing in Taiwan now created the world's largest semiconductor fabricating foundry named TSMC (Taiwan

Semiconductor Manufacturing Company) occupying over 50% of the world's foundry market with one of the most advanced fabricating technology in system semiconductors. That means over half of the semiconductor design houses all over the world have their chips fabricated in Taiwan. This is a typical pincer movement of German general Rommel's tank troops. Such isolated penetration needs the support from secure supply lines. Without it the brave penetrators will wither away. Taiwan put too many eggs on one basket, TSMC, which occupies 35% of the capitalization value of the nation's stock market.[77]

Samsung Electronics started the foundry business ten years ago and occupied only 16% of the global foundry orders until last year whereas TSMC takes 53%. But slow technology progress of TSMC in 3-nano chips and GAA (gate all around) technology, which Samsung started mass production in June 2023, and the high chip-price policy of TSMC threatens great clients like IBM, AMI, QUALCOMM, and NVidia away to Samsung. Geopolitical risks from the Beijing government scares away the chip buyers

---

[77] Hong Hai, known as Foxcon that assembles most of mobile phones for Apple takes another 25% of Taipei Exchange. Together the two subcontract companies cover over half of Taiwan's market capitalization value.

of the world.

Taiwan's domestic market for TSMC products and services is insignificant in size compared to the TSMC capacity. A substantial part of the demand came from mainland China but due to the American prohibition of semiconductor exports to China keeping the market share became very hard.

Taiwan wrongly believed that the world will protect it from Chinese invasion because the fall of Taiwan will disturb the global economy seriously. They called it the Semiconductor Shield and angered many Americans for the irresponsible attitude for national security. The world is looking for the evacuation of TSMC from Taiwan instead and criticizes Taiwan's ungrateful attitude for goodwill of the free world.

# X. Economic Development and Human Value

## People Values Differ by Countries

If one has to select one lesson to be derived from the South Korean experience of continuous long-term economic development, it should be the rise in human value of the people who made it happen. We know who the prominent heroes were in our developmental history and I will not repeat them. Enough has been written and said about the heroic odysseys of Syngman Rhee, Chung Hee Park, Byung Chul Lee, Joo Young Chung, and many lesser titans.

Here I want to talk about the *people*. With the people, I mean the men on the street who were serfs and slaves to a foreign government and to land-owning compatriots. They turned to independent farmers and workers, as well as entrepreneurs. These people, who classified themselves as a middle class from the beginning, are the parents who didn't hesitate to borrow tens of thousand dollars for the competitive education of their children. Their children, who became the new middle class of Korea, send 30 dollars every month to help UNICEF to feed the starving children of Africa. This same middle class now owns one or more apartment blocks in Seoul or in suburb that costs frequently more than a million US dollars each.[78]

In my own lifetime, the children who walked 3 to 5 miles every day to commute to school and had no electricity at home became grandparents of kids studying at Harvard, Berkeley, Julliard, and INSEAD, Fontainebleau, and became parents of children who live in million dollar apartments in Seoul driving expensive German cars. Korean workers became expensive.[79] Korean corporations who employ these expensive Korean workers bet billions of dollars in equipment and machines for these workers to work with, and come up with outputs worth many more billions of dollars in semi-conductors, lithium batteries that make

---

[78] This is an important statement that has to be verified. We will see more on this estimation soon.

[79] According to the reports of labor union of the Hyundai Motor Company, the average annual wages paid to the union members including bonus payments surpassed 100 million won (roughly equal to 85,000 UD dollars) mark in 2018.

cars run 1000 km without recharging and LNG carriers that maintain the temperature of -170 degree Celsius. The Russian cut-off of the Nord Stream gas pipe lines forced the frantic Europeans to place huge orders to Korea for these LNG carriers but the dockyards are full for five years.

Relative human value is a delicate and dangerous concept. Insurance companies set up their own actuarial formula for calculating the value of human lives to determine the compensations in case of accidents. Whichever way one looks at it, we cannot avoid facing the differentiation in the assessment of human values in some form in all communities. I don't believe in equal human *economic value*. That is a noble question of political philosophy. But this book is about how to raise the economic values of the people of a country. That starts from accepting differences in the human economic value of different countries.

It is reported that in the morning of 2021.05.19 Israel army spent tens of million dollars for protecting their citizens by operating the Iron Dome, an assembly of a protective sets of missiles that intercepted incoming enemy rockets. Palestinian army spent less than 5 million dollars in sending the rockets in order to attack Tel Aviv. However, nobody is complaining about the apparent overspending by the Israeli side. Israelites obviously believe the lives of their citizens are worth the money. All men may be created equal but are not economically equal.

Neither President Park, nor Chairman B.C. Lee sold a single article at the swampy Indonesian jungles, extremely competitive European markets, or tightened a bolt under the sizzling sun of Saudi deserts. These people, the millions of modern Cinderella did. Raising the values of your own people should be the prime goal of any economic development efforts. Failure in raising economic values of your own people instantly manifests in the form of social unrest and vehement opposition to further investment and economic growth. We call that the middle income country stagnation. Opponents of growth take such noble causes as environmental protection and social equity as their weapons, while in reality, whether intended or not, they are promoting continuous mass poverty. Poor neighborhood is where their ideology ferments. In Korea some environmentalists were discovered as spies of communist neighbor.

Making your own compatriots' value higher is more

of an art than a science. Ministries of Economic Planning, Labor, Education, and Industry and Trade all believe this is their turf, frequently with conflicting objectives between themselves. Improvement in human values may not bring an immediate appreciation. In fact, people tend to show more greed as they get better off. But it is the best point to focus on policy objectives. I've never seen a Human Value Party, but one may run for the presidential office on this platform. That will ensure better focus and coordination between policies for the candidate.

## Turning People into Scarce Resources

Education works best in raising human values in any country. In spite of unending and ubiquitous criticism of their public education system, successful academic records still is and perhaps will be one of the quickest ways to get the recognition one wishes. I never saw corporate and university recruiters demanding personal history deleting educational background. By reading a candidate's history of education, we justify our assumption on what an applicant can and cannot do. At least we get to know what supplementary education my applicant needs. Falling in the box of the *employable* group makes the roads ahead very wide. Unfortunately, too many countries fail to produce enough of these employable youngsters. In fact, some countries are busy in stealing manpower with advanced technologies from foreign corporations. Chinese semiconductor companies are recruiting thousands of Taiwanese engineers from advanced companies like TSMC, not all legally. An education system sensitive to corporate needs can go a long way in raising the value of your own people.

Korea's culture of excessively competitive education produced over 800,000 high school graduates every year during most of the high growth period and more than 85% of them enrolled at some form of tertiary educational institution. We were worried quite seriously about this abnormally top-heavy structure of education. It turned out that we were myopic. Korean corporations were able to train the graduates as officers of companies and assigned them to projects all over the world, whereas our university graduates recruited the working force locally and trained them to suit their local purpose. It was a shortcut for raising human value in hindsight. We didn't plan it like Adolf Hitler who secretively raised over ten thousand cadets with his quota of one army division granted by the Paris League 1919, but tiger mums of Korea collectively found this shortcut to higher and more valuable use of their children in multinational corporations of future Korea. Our limited population size could have restricted our growth capacity, without the lucky obsession for higher education among Koreans. Unlike army divisions, our wage-earning mercenary divisions of multinational corporations can be lawfully organized anywhere in the world and equip them with high-powered machines, instead of machine guns, to suit the local economic goals. And local governments welcomed our effort to recruit their people as our private soldiers in our expedition to conquer the global markets.

We have 0.7% of the global population in Korea, but we produce 75% of all the memory chips that the world needs now. We produce nearly 100% of the LNG tankers, LNG-driven ships, and ice-breaking ships used at the North Pole Routes to Europe from East Asia, and 55% of the global lithium batteries, etc. The small Korean national territory is rapidly running out of space and labor supply. Korean corporations found the solution in direct overseas investments that produce electronic goods, automobiles and a wide range of mechanical components in Eastern Europe. Semiconductors and mobile phones, petroleum and petrochemical plants use the spaces of South East Asia, and automobile components and assembly, electronic goods and semiconductors found space in the Indian subcontinent. All of them use the locally recruited mercenaries and trained them as good private soldiers and our grandchildren fill in the officer positions.

## Urban Redevelopment Projects with No Budget

Amateurish real estate market policy of the socialistic government of Korea intervened with the market price mechanism by massively raising windfall gains taxes charged on house sales, and integrated property ownership taxes to cool the hot property market. Naturally this additional tax burdens were shifted forward by the property owners to buyers in a this hot seller's market. The market price of their assets rose dramatically producing over 3 millionaire families in the city of Seoul, its suburban cities, and regional metropolis which together has about three quarters of the total population of Korea. According to news reports, the average price of a unit of apartment in Seoul just passed 1.1 billion won of Korean currency that is almost exactly 1 million US dollars.[80]

KOSIS, the Korean government statistics agency site reports that there are 21.5 million families in Korea, and total number of housing units is 18.5 million, among which 11.66 million units are modern apartments and 3.89 million is independent houses. Rented apartments by owners of more than one unit, is roughly 800,000 units and this figure should be deducted from 3 million. But the 3.89 million independent houses in average carry price tags higher than the apartments, therefore more than compensate for the loss of rented apartments. Furthermore Korean middle class families own other assets.

---

[80] The Ministry of National Territory keeps the real-time database of real estate contracts made within the country by automatic and mandatory registration. There are total of 11.66 million apartment units (I rounded up the numbers) in Korea as of January 2022 and 8 autonomous and semi-autonomous cities have 4.530 million of them (including 1.5 million for Seoul), and the most–populous province, Geong Gi Do has 3.031 million. According to the Herald Economy, one of the local Korean economic newspapers, (Jan 19,2022) 66.9% of the apartments located in Seoul were valued at over 900,000,000 won(roughly equal to 770,000 US dollars) and nearly half of it (31%) has price tags over 15 billion won (1.28 million USD). In other words, little over a million families are living in a property that is over 770 thousand dollars. Using half this ratio for Geong Gi Province and the regional metropolis another two million units are priced over this mark.

The Bank of Korea releases its estimation of the Korean National Balance Sheet once in three years with interim interpolation as annual reports. It is rich in information regarding the pure asset values and liabilities of Korean citizens and corporations. According to the report of 2022, the gross asset value of Korean citizens, excluding corporations and governments, is a total of 10,717 trillion won (roughly equal to USD 9.160 trillion), which is consisted of 5,344 trillion won for residents, 2,419 trillion won for non-resident real estates, 1,968 trillion won for cash and deposits, 886 trillion won for stocks and investment funds. *The net asset value* per family is 512.2 million won, roughly equal to USD 437,607. If we add this net asset value, the 3 million families with assets over 770,000 will rise rapidly. For convenience's sake let us agree that well *over 3 million Korean families are millionaires.*[81]

---

[81] Korea experienced three currency reforms (actually replacements); one in 1945 to cleanse the overprinting of Korean money by the treasury of defeated Japan, two in 1950 to neutralize the overprinting by the North Korean Army who captured the Bank of Korea, in Seoul, and three in 1962 by the new military government who thought that stashed cash of rich merchants can be mobilized for industrial purpose. I was serving in the army then and my own economics professor at the Seoul National University, Mr. Hee Bum Park, was recruited for the execution of this reform as Deputy Minister of Finance. He was young, ambitious, and radical, but the result was so miserable that he was dismissed. Since then the same currency is used until now.

At around that time, Korea's per capita GDP is estimated at around US 100 dollars. This

Inflating human values with-property price hikes is not a desirable policy, especially when it is at the expense of the victims who do not own property. It will devalue by itself in time. In city-states inflated rental income can be major source-of GDP increases, but a manufacturing economy like Korea cannot afford the inflated cost of land and offices. Inflated rental income usually inflates only human greed and expectations for more rises, which is very dangerous. Therefore most of the sound- minded policymakers and economists try to dismiss this route of asset building as a serious tool in reaching prosperity, especially in a country that suffers a low birth rate of babies.

However, behind the property bubbles there exist real causes for further increases in property prices such as the expectation of continuous growth of the Korean economy, shortage in supply of available land, values coming from

figure grew to about 32,000 US dollars now, about 320 times increase. A typical high school teacher earned about won 3000, which is about 10 US dollars, then. A typical three-bedroom house at a suburb of Seoul (3-4 km from the city center) sold at about 1 million won, and a second-hand GE refrigerator brought in by returning diplomats commanded about the same price. A three-bedroom modern flat in a typical 30-floor apartment building at the same location now costs about one billion won; a thousand times increase. The national average of residential units costs about half of this example but it is reported there are more than 3 million apartment units that cost about and over this billion-won mark.

the better environment, easy access to school and private education, access to mass transits, better buildings, better facilities such as elevators and parks, and many other. Most importantly the fact that the property owners were able to shift their tax burden forward implies that the whole community regards the present real estate price is not a bubble. The boom finally bust in late 2022 and property price actually declined since the peak by about 40% but many investors are waiting for the market signal of an upward cycle. Unlike the comfortable American residences built on vast suburban lands, Korean apartments are mostly built on the hot neighborhoods with mass transit, schools, shopping facilities, hospitals, and parks, that makes the potential supply restricted and expensive.

Korean cities are built on lands owned by thousands of owners with delicately winding and twining border lines between rice paddies that existed there for over a thousand years. Drawing and building any straight-lined roads and streets is bound to automatically step on somebodies valuable property whose owners are extremely sensitive where a new road is passing, ready to sue the government or housing authorities. The city planners of authoritarian communist countries never had this problem. But in a market economy, where the sanctity of private ownership of property is guaranteed by the constitution, and the separation of power between administration and judiciary is effective, It proved to be the best policy to appease the farmers and owners of tiny pieces of urban property by taking measures that raise their property values, that is a form of legally permissible bribing.

Municipal governments or housing authorities drew an attractive plan of the new town that has parks, lakes, trees, lawns, schools, medical clinics, and shopping centers all within the boundary of a new apartment community, and the apartments are fully equipped with all the modern amenities; electric power supply, elevators, drinking water supply, sewerage system, shared security systems for the entire community, wifi internet connections (used to be community TV antenna), individual cooling systems, shared supply of hot water connected to Ondol, the Korean traditional floor-heating system, by regional power company burning the methane gas extracted from the pre-sorted trashes. Landowners agree quickly to the land mobilization agreement for the joint land development program. The conversion of the land-use zoning from individual housing or farm land to high-density residential zone raises the land values by ten folds at the least.

At the beginning, such new town projects used only lands owned by local governments but that is very rare in Korea. But the magnificent windfall gains earned by the success of neighboring new towns provoked owners of pieces of land or residences in the urban ghetto area instantly, and they organized cooperatives to conduct the complex process for getting permissions required for the urban redevelopment battle. It is so popular that it takes at least five years from the initiation of the cooperative's joint development projects to get permissions to pool the land and redevelop private lands. If you add the construction period, ten years is safe to assume before you move into your brand new apartment with a price tag several times that of your old home. This is possible because the new high-rise apartment buildings, 20 to 50 stories, produce many new homes to sell to nonmembers of the cooperatives at the post-development market price.

This makes old members afford bigger and more modern spaces and awards the contracted developer attractive profits. It is all possible because the floor–space ratio[82] is raised by eight times or more, and the value of their real estate shot up like rockets as soon as full permission for the integrated redevelopment plan is obtained. Cooperative members pay some fees that are more than recovered by the dividend of the high market price of his new home. The surplus space is sold to the public who responded with enthusiasm. Generous laws and policy of floor-space ratio enabled the project owners to create huge margins[83] after covering the cost of land purchase, building and trimming, and sales taxes for selling the apartment spaces to new residents.

The art of urban redevelopment projects without budgets begins here. The ministry of the national territory and the city governments should determine the price of apart-

---

[82] It is the total floor space of the entire new building divided by the legally occupied land size. If the land size is 3000 square meters and the total sum of floor space of the building is 30,000 square meters, then the ratio is 10. For commercial property, this ratio can rise over 10. For residences, it is typically 2.5 or below but for 'densely multi-occupied residences' (sorry for the official jargon) that means apartments, 5 to 8 are awarded.

[83] One presidential candidate, J.M.Lee, while he was the mayor of a suburban city of Seoul, designed this sort of urban renewal program that netted over huge profit margins to the project owners. He is under prosecutor's investigation on multiple crimes but he insists that he will remain as the government party candidate until he is formally charged and proven guilty.

ments (upper limits actually) low enough to keep a healthy inflow of new non-member applicants to buy new apartments. But it should also be high enough to cover the rising cost of land, which is pushed upward by the very success of these renewal projects, and other costs. The upper limit of the floor-space ratio is already exhausted and reflected in the calculation of income for the project owner. The most powerful policy tool is the control of the upper limit of mortgage loans to homeowners new and old, by trading banks.

Almost always this pool of lending resources of banks seems exhausted in Korea, for banks are always in short supply of mortgage-lending funds reflecting the popularity of residential investment. Total outstanding household mortgage loans is 80% of the size of GDP and became a sensitive news item. Government controls the size of mortgage lending by issuing lending limits of banks or the loan/income ratio. This is the second policy tool after the speed of permissions. The third and most powerful tool is the control of special property sales tax, a windfall tax on the gains of property value. I should not get into details but the government can boost or cool down the housing market by controlling these tools and more. By steeply raising the graduation of progressive property income tax, the government is discouraging speculators.

The excessive borrowing by the household sector, most of which is residential mortgage lending, is getting close to the Korean GDP. That proves among other things that the Korean property market is pushed high enough. To cool down the real estate market, the government started to raise the housing supply. Through public development corporations and selected private construction companies, new towns are under construction at the outer periphery of Seoul, which will put 2 million more new apartments in the market within two to three years. They will be 15 to 20 kilometers further out from the existing new towns and will be connected by electric rails. The land development cost will be provided by the private and public development companies for profit, not the tax money.

Korea has a unique mortgage lending system called *Jeonse* that has existed since the early part of its growth. It is a system in which the tenant plays the role of the bank by lending 80% of the property value to the landlord. That means anybody who has 20% of the property market value in cash was able to purchase a property, put it on Jeonse, and enjoy the high inflation of residential prices. Tenants are happy that they use the house almost free because the entire amount is returned at the end of Jeonse contract. Long before our modern banking system adopted the long-term mortgage lending system, our private residential market operated using this substitute for long-term mortgages. The important thing is that this system helped build up a comfortable middle class that has become the bastion of our democracy and the source of stable growth for another half-century.

## The Winners

The happy winners are the residents in the new apartments. In the case of Banpo district and some other similar districts in most of the metropolitan Seoul price of their assets rose over 1000 folds during the last 60 years. And in Gyeong Gi province, surrounding the metropolitan Seoul, over 3.0 million apartment units were built on former rice paddies, and property prices rose by similar rates during the last half century. For the whole country Korean construction industry built over 11.6 million apartments during this period, building 220 thousand apartment units a year on average, as well as other independent housing units every year.

In about thirty years, the typical Korean middle-class family who owned assets barely worth 1,000 dollars became owners of assets worth on average close to one million dollars, and even five million dollars for lucky ones living in districts of Gangnam, Socho, Songpa, Yongsan, Mapo, and Seong Dong. The lowest class of residence in Seoul starts with 500,000 dollars price tag. The point is by a clever combination of strong housing demand, conducive government policy initiations, and strong and resilient construction industry participation, one can achieve three objectives simultaneously; successful urban renewal projects with no special budget, raising a strong domestic construction industry, and most importantly creating millions of domestic middle-class millionaires through owning urban housing units. Compare this number to the total membership of the most militant labor union of Korea which is little over a million. North Korean conspiracy to subvert South Korean polity cannot win, for there are too many happy Koreans enjoying their wealth.[84]

Building residential units is only a part of the construction industry, which has to build plants, ports, airports, office buildings, schools, exhibition halls etc in and out of Korea. But the huge domestic residential-building industry is a strong anti-recession policy tool, for it comes with a large number of specialized outsourcing subcontractor groups for each construction company of principal contracts, and the subcontractor group comes with huge employment effects. The total contribution of the Korean construction industry to GDP, which was 17% at the peak, comes close to that of the Korean manufacturing industry, which is 21%. In most OECD countries, the weight of the construction industry usually is less than 10%.

But the real winner is the government which owns the LH Corporation[85] that clears land, connects all the water, sewerage, power, and communication systems, and sells

---

[84] The League of Democratic Labor Unions, which is very militant, has a registered member of 1,134,000 members. According to Mr. Jang Yub Hwang, the North Korean answer to Karl Marx who invented the Ju Che Theory, and escaped to the South, there are 40,000 North Korean spy moles in South Korea living quietly. The list of voluntary surrenders is endless but the government cannot disclose it to protect them.

[85] It is the Land and Housing Corporation of Korea, a public company owned and run by the government. It started as the law-cost housing supplier for low-income class but these days it competes with private construction companies and sets the pace of market signals.

*at profit* by reflecting all the land development costs based on the market land price. The urban renewal program is applied from Seoul and the vicinity to all the small agricultural and fishery towns with the same legal and economic frameworks. By keeping the property and housing market upbeat and keeping the living experience in high-rise buildings comfortable, and by forcing provision of parks, schools, shopping, and easy access by railroads, the government saved billions of dollars in constructing modern cities on the same sites of old shabby low-quality houses near 100-years old, mostly by the private residential investments of the people, that is financed by commercial bank mortgages.

The Ministry of National Territory spends annually about 3.8% of the national budget on building rails; subway urban metros, high-speed rails (350 km per hour), and GTX(grand-underground transport at 50 meters deep underground). Lion's share of it goes to connecting eight major population centers like Seoul and Busan with surrounding commuter's bed towns and helped raise the property values of suburban apartments in parallel to the property price of Seoul. Taxpayers paid roughly 33% of GDP in tax, and 3.8% of it was spent on raising the property prices owned by middle-low income bracket taxpayers who couldn't afford property in Seoul and commute to cities. That's a good politics of balanced national territorial development. It gives hope to all Koreans that someday they can own a million-dollar property.

Everybody, including the IMF, worries about the excess borrowing by Korean households, which is mostly mortgage borrowing. All the household borrowings are backed by real estate assets and if the market prices of these assets bust then the worry is justified. The present socialist government of Korea hated the unearned middle-class windfall gains rising, and stopped issuing permissions for new urban renewal projects for two and a half years. As a result the new supply of large-scale apartment buildings virtually stopped now. And the housing price rose more together with the detested middle-class windfall gains. The government regularly apologizes for failing to arrest the rising prices of urban apartments and the household debt that keeps on rising in tandem. Media constantly criticize the housing price policies but I am certain that all of the bureaucrats, reporters, and consumers are enjoying the rising asset values of their own homes, planning their next visit to Europe or Australia with their families. We need a standard to compare the national household debt to declare it too high or too low. We need a national balance sheet of assets and debts.[86]

I hope readers by now are agreeable to the importance of building national assets not only in the form of huge plants, buildings, roads, and parks, but also in market values of privately owned residences that rise in parallel to the economic growth rate. Huge plants cannot be owned by individual citizens, but they can own small parts of expensive

---

[86] This strategy of brooding millions of millionaires through the rezoning of urban-center ghettos requires extreme care, for it is open to massive windfall incomes to powerful and crooked. In a country ruled by one communist party, the entire family of party apparatus can join in sharing the games hunted. Some lucky citizens can earn some windfall but most of the wealth created are distributed within the loyal gangs and there is no social fuss, for the party controls the media. Most of the history of Japan under the new 'peace constitution' since WWII is ruled by the conservative Jiminto (Free-Democratic Party) at the top supported by industry, media, and Yakusa(organized crime network). The system is very similar to China where the party controls the media. CCP uses the police force and Jimin To uses Yakusa for domesticating media. Scandals of massive profit made by urban real estate rezoning and related trials are not reported in China although the evidence stand tall everywhere. Such scandals are occasionally reported in Japan but never heard of indictment for rezoning scandals. At this very moment, a presidential candidate of the majority party of Korea is about to be summoned by the prosecutor's office for investigation of massive potentially unlawful profits made by the cronies of this gentleman at a city where he was the mayor when the rezoning and land sales took place. Opposition party demands setting up a special independent prosecutor's office for this investigation as the law requires.

residential buildings. The return can be far more attractive than their investments in securities.

So many governments and leaders neglect the task of creating a healthy, stable, and large middle class. So many conservative intellectuals seem to believe that building huge Jaebols in developing economies is a policy of *necessary evil* and that *relative deprivation of the nation's majority* is inevitable and fair price to pay for rapid growth in market economy. The world is full of examples where this wrong hypothesis put into practice. Policy that creates many world class high-tech corporations is not an evil, and hopeless sense of deprivation by the middle class is not necessary either. A developing country should create more companies like Samsung and LG than Korea did, and a *healthy, stable, wide-spread middle class with satisfying private asset values* will prevent middle-class alienation and help building a well-functioning democracy. There is no historical example of any nation that achieved lasting prosperity without democratic free market economy and healthy middle class with significant assets. The real estate price curve of any society rises and falls but only in a shrinking sick economy the curve dives down to the south-east. In normal healthy developing economies, the curve rises to the northeast fluctuating around the trend line. Only those countries where the majority of middle class enjoys the rising value of the property can sustain their growth.

In America, this shared prosperity is called making the *American dream* come true. The number of suburban middle class outnumbers the other class. Early twentieth-century growth of industrial America gave the basis to achieve American dreams that other advanced countries couldn't match. Supporters of law and order easily outnumber the disrupters. Middle-class asset building is not a smooth process and fluctuates with occasional mortgage failures even in America, but the high productivity of American industries successfully supported this structure of massive participation by suburbanites in sharing the fruits of American wealth building. America succeeded in making the American Dream a reachable dream for many. Unlike the China Dream which is an imperial dream for the nation; the American dream is for the free individuals.

In this second part of this volume, we investigated how Korea succeeded in creating a bridgehead in the land of

HMPE industries where only the best and strongest corporations play in tightly woven *cartels* based on accumulated trusts and reliabilities. Against unlikely odds and through painful economic crises, Korean Jaebols grew to a global scale and became the object of admiration as well as hatred by the Korean people. This love-hate relationship of Korean companies with their own people only intensified as they grew into technological juggernauts and humbled many giants and even governments of the world.

Korean middle class could have easily turned *against more growth that only exacerbates inequality*. Existential threats from hostile neighbors and the Korean dream of the ever-increasing value of middle-class assets kept them in support of the market system that lays golden eggs for them. Technology nationalism of Korean Jaebols provided the wherewithal for building effective deterrence against foreign aggressions. Nearly all the Korean HMPE companies have been producing some form of weapons for several decades and now they are capable of producing export quality weapons of high technology. Jaebols became tools for wealth creation as well as peace.

Korean middle class is aware that their high individual economic value depends on the democratic system and market economy and they show their support by joining street demonstrations whenever it is in danger. By keeping the country in peace, and by keeping the people's value high, Korean People and Jaebols became partners sharing the same goal. Koreans found that they satisfied all the necessary and sufficient conditions for sustained growth; ie. Peace, Freedom of Democracy, the Market Economy. The strong middle class supports all these goals.

# Is Korea Going Anywhere?

# XI. Koreans Think We Just Began

## An Effective Skeleton for Nation Building

We analyzed the modern history of Korea by focusing on the important changes that entailed more impact in building the nation. Needless to say, there are other changes that must have left a significant impact. But the assumption this book makes is that the other changes, for example, the modernization of bureaucratic organizations and administration, are derivative changes that followed the corporate sector leadership that changed faster and more dynamically. The object of this book is not to list all the important changes Korea made. It is to build a skeleton of developmental experience that can be repeated by latecomers.

The first and foremost base structure for nation-building

is peace and security. Not all countries need a strong army and military industries to keep the peace. Devoting close to 3% of the GDP to national defense is a substantial burden. If one is lucky enough to have somebody to keep you safe and away from a war on your territory like Taiwan believes it is, it is a very unusual blessing. If one is as unlucky as Korea, then there is only one way to follow; turn the crisis into an opportunity by nurturing your own strong military industry.

Democracy, the second base structure, is a very fragile system for a country which has to fight, while at the same time economically grow. Korean media and press was not invincible under the pressures of the power and money but was largely successful in keeping our politicians becoming overtly corrupt. That helped a lot. For a country constantly under threat, people are easily tempted to think that editorial attitude of the press should always be complementary with the national goals of survival and avoid criticizing the government policies that may debilitate the social stability. Japanese press still keeps this attitude. But if the press turns its face the other way when power goes corrupt, the middle income class will become cynical to further development and the long journey for creating national wealth stops. En-tire national power and talents will be dedicated to cheating the system of law and distort the system for immediate per-sonal gains.

An effective market economy guarantees private prop-erty ownership of capital goods. That is another name for the freedom of establishing and managing modern corpora-tions. This is the third base structure of successful nation-building and directly contrasts with the common ownership of the communist system. Examples of their failure are so ubiquitous, that we do not need to repeat them. The rule of survival of the least cost and best quality in the market competition works wonders in strengthening the economy that only those who actually experienced it can appreciate.

When the three base structures are solidly built, you need the players to put on the stage. The main players are your own uneducated and poor people without much skill, but they are your most valuable natural resources as well as the very party that should be made happy by your ef-forts of building prosperity. The second group of players is the merchants who have to be persuaded to build modern corporations and be turned into billionaires. They usually know how to make profits better than you know. Give them what they need and they will do their work if you can keep their corruption within a boundary and don't let yourself be a party of corruption alliance. That's not easy but it is essential that your polity should be above corporation owners, even if you have to put them in jail for a while occasionally.

That brings us to You. You are the project master of great nation-building. You are the select members of the highest intellectual group, the moving forces of future studies, and the reflection of the Zeit Geist. You are spread everywhere that needs your help. You enjoy the respect of the people and community. At times you push soldiers to rule the country because the traditional entrenchment of indifference, despair, and generalized corruption is beyond repair. When a revolution is needed, you lead the mob in front. When restraint and tolerance are needed, you become the tranquilizer. But when the tough military rule reveals its limitation, you drove the soldiers away from the stage without hesitation and gave the people the right to rule themselves. It is a great blessing that your country has you. You are born in the classrooms, battlefields, international markets, and laboratories.

The development history of Korea can be summed up as the sequential introduction of Mandatory Education systems; the Land Reforms and the post-war Hyperinflation; the Military Coup de tat; the forceful execution of the Five-year Economic Plans that turned the country wide-open; the creation of General Trading Houses to connect small domestic producers to the global markets in professional way; the series of Oil Price Shocks and the birth of the Korean HMPE industries; the birth and brilliant growth of the uniquely Korean Jaebols; equally unique birth of the Korean Technological Nationalism and Technological Independence; the twist of the Cold War that turned China the most favored child of America and the frightening sense of isolation and neglect felt by South Koreans that forced the birth of Korean Weapons Industry; the return to Democracy when the Soviet Union started to show cracks on the wall of Communist edifice; Economic Crisis that drove weaker Jaebols and companies down to the drain, and made the remaining corporate sector far more dynamic and resilient;

the commencement of Semiconductor industry in Korea at a time when the world started to be connected by WWW and Internet; the flood of digitalization of corporation management, government administration, military operations, and family lives. These are the main parts of the structure and skeleton that Korea built. Clearly, all of it represents Korea's responses to the need of the time without any blueprint. We didn't know how to make blueprints. What we called plans were just the list of wishful targets but we have shown the tenacity to make the wishes a reality. We called that learning by doing.

In the meantime, the Fallacy of Supply-Chain Optimization hollowed the manufacturing sectors of the most advanced nations. This was hidden until the corona pandemic exposed this scandalous neglect of the manufacturing capability of nearly all European countries. This impotence was further exposed by the shameless Russian Invasion of Ukraine. The world's second most powerful nation, Russia, and its duplicator, China are proven as no more than paper tigers equipped with useless inferior weapons. The corrupt Russian military officers, weapons makers, and party officers stole the military budgets at every stage of the military acquisition process whenever they can. This epidemic of corruption lasted a whole century since the Bolshevik Revolution in 1919. China's military and party members stole no less and China almost never paid for technological transfer, therefore the target-hitting precision of their weapons is not much higher than random shooting as has been discovered in the Pakistani-India frontier clash. Consequently, a surprising fact became known that in today's world there are only two reliable high-tech weapons exporters in the world who can deliver within time requested, the USA and Korea. Luckily two are both in the free-democratic camp.

This totally unexpected circumstance provides a testing opportunity of national survival structure that Korea built. Korea was born under the context of the Cold War and fought a surrogate war for the ideological contestants. We didn't win the war but we won by economic and political development that our adversary cannot even compare.[87] Russia asks us for help, publicly and privately, while at the

---

[87] North Korea doesn't want to admit that they lost the conflict by the development of a nuclear bombs including the delivery system. We had to develop a weapon of counterattack called Chunmoo-5 that flies at speed of 10-Mach and carries explosives as powerful as 1/4 times the Hiroshima bomb without any radio activities.

same time threatening lest we provide our high-precision weapons to Ukraine. Poland sent nearly all its weapons to Ukraine in aid, because Poland shares a borderline with Russia and Bello Russ as long as Ukraine and feels an intense danger of Russian invasion. Poland signed a contract to buy 980 K2 tanks, near 600 K9 auto-loading mobile howitzers, and 48 K50 fighter aircraft. Korean plants of tanks, fighter aircraft, and mobile auto-howitzers are busy with visitors from Poland, Romania, Slovakia, Finland, and Baltic three. To assure early delivery, one of them sent 30% of the total payment as contract money. Their national survival is at stake. More than half of the weapons contracted will be assembled in Poland due to labor sabotages at the Korean plants. We did not plan or want to come to this sensitive point of responsibility. Frankly, we are scared. Planning Korea's future is not enough anymore. The world is envisaging the end to the hundred-year-old Cold War. Is it the end of history as Fukuyama claims? Or is it the beginning of chaotic and simultaneous clashes of small powers all around the world? The easy time when the world was a stable background to us is over now. We became an important element of the background itself.

# Democracy and the Korean Development

Korea rushed breathlessly all the way to advanced country status with virtually no time or opportunity to sit down and think. This new status *does not fit us well* and we feel very uncomfortable. We have gone through major crises and adjustments whenever the global economy demanded it. During oil price crises, we were lucky to find the right strategy of ramming through the Middle Eastern dollar boxes with construction and engineering contracts, but during foreign exchange shortage crises that crushed several Asian economies in 1996-7, we were humbled by the power of global financial muscle, and we were blamed for being morally hazardous as if we planned not to pay the debt back from the beginning.[88]

The Asian economic crisis of 1997, which Koreans called the IMF crisis as if this institution caused the crisis, was the right time for us to stop dashing and start thinking. The crisis came barely 10 years after South Korea returned

---

[88] I wonder whether they really believed in what they said then. If we really planned from the beginning not to pay our debts, we were immoral and criminal, period. Whenever I stood in front of small and large audiences who came to listen to what a speaker from a morally hazardous country would say, I had great difficulty in deciding what sort of facial expression I should maintain. I knew I was not immoral but not proud either.

to a free democratic government with a properly functioning National Assembly, direct presidential election, free press, and labor unions. Unfortunately for Korea and the system of democracy, the freely elected government was inept, ineffective, irrational, ignorant, and unprepared, especially compared to the dreaded but efficient militaristic governments of the immediate past.

We practically invited the foreign exchange shortage crisis. The per capita GDP of Korea, then, was just below USD 10,000, and this marked the threshold of the door to joining the OECD. President Y.S. Kim needed this political achievement of obtaining OECD membership, and had to exaggerate our GDP by overvaluing the exchange ratio; i.e. 820 won to a dollar, whereas it blew up to 1,800 won to a dollar when the crisis came. Korea had to borrow 66 billion dollars from the IMF standby emergency reserves under the condition that any private nonperforming loan accounts of Korean domestic banks to Jaebols be immediately closed. This caused more than half of the top 30 Jaebols to go bankrupt. Furthermore, the government budget was forcefully balanced immediately and the central bank was forbidden from printing money for the government. This pushed the domestic interest rate to jump to 23%. More liquidation followed.

I am not fair to him, because President Kim, Young Sam, according to his personal confession, had to spend virtually all of his political capital in dismembering the notorious Hana Hoe, which was the exclusive army elite officers' club whose members were convinced that Korea was not ready for civilian government yet and is rumored to planning a new coup. President Y.S. Kim set the understructure of Korea's democracy for sustained development by permanently uprooting further military intervention on our democratic process. Furthermore, he forcefully enacted the Real-Name Account System, which instantly revealed the true size of all the private wealth of Koreans, and the biggest tax loophole was closed. This financial revolution was implemented by his conservative government. Japan still allows false name accounts at the banks in 2023. Korean government budget is balanced but Japanese government budget deficit mounted to 300% of GDP. *It was the democratically elected government that fumbled at crisis, not the democratic system.* But the pain of the massive number of corporate liquidations was enough to cause nostalgia for past authoritarian management.

There was a small Piketty commotion recently in the Korean National Assembly. A politician of socialist inclination quoted the Bank of Korea report showing the Piketty index rose from 7.4 to 8.8 in ten years since 2012 blaming worsening inequality of income distribution in Korea. The ratio between the rate of return on capital and the rate of growth of output and income is reported to have risen and that is the complaint. Mr. Piketty warned that if the rate of the return of capital of a country exceeds the economic growth rate, then it will 'radically undermine the meritocratic values on which democratic societies survive.' What he is saying is that a high Piketty Ratio is bad for a country. A generous abuse of words attracts politicians who love to whip the coach instead of the horse to speed up.

There is no question that the super-rich are getting richer faster than the lowest income class in Korea, or anywhere for that matter. And this disparity increases when economy grows faster for faster growth is associated with more investment. The only way for the capital income not to grow is to give up investment and growth. And as technology advances, capital investment per labor rises fast and the labor productivity and wages rise as well. We called that the rise in human economic value. The only way for this ratio not to rise is to give up technology growth. This is why the Piketty ratio is higher in advanced countries and higher in economic up cycles than in crises. Korea has many other worries that are more important than the Piketty ratio.

China managed the introduction of the market system by the Communist government with a combination of brutal police intervention and this economy is called the *state capitalism*. That is an oxymoron. Capitalism is based on private industrial property ownership that is in contrast with state ownership except under very special circumstances such as a natural monopoly industry. It pains me when I hear economic *specialists* in the media comment on the *state capitalism* of China as if it is a viable ideology. We saw the private market economy in China succeed in economic growth even under the communist government, but not because of it. The strength of the market economy came from the competitive energy of the people. The competitive spirit of the Chinese people made the market successful, not the CCP dictatorship. CCP began a campaign of discouraging or preventing the growth of privately-owned industries such as Ma Win's Alibaba. The excuse is that the strong private sector interferes with the progress of the communist party ideals. Under democracy wealth owned by the people is a success indicator but under communism wealth owned by the people is a deterrence to the party ideology and should be restrained. Under democracy, people, corporations, and the government dash for prosperity helping each other, but in communism, only the government should run while others are advised to remain as spectators.

China has an amazing national pool of talent and a system that tolerates or even encourages, acts of copying whatever that is revealed to be valuable. In front of the gargantuan flow of its history and national development drama, this misplaced talent and tolerance may look meaningless. But to the eyes of this author, this culture of illegal replication and national-scale piracy is the most serious detriment that prevents China from becoming one of the global leaders, which it deserves to be.

Like opium that crushed the Ching dynasty in the middle of the 19th century, this illegal duplication has become addictive throughout the nation because the return is instant and big where imports of originals are prohibited by government. Who would spend millions of dollars and thousands of hours in hard toil for research? The Chinese people are extremely talented in science and technology but if the culture that gives better rewards to cheaters continues, China will never become the leader because for number one there is nobody to copy.

Secondly, this culture encourages people to break laws. China has laws that protect intellectual property but if the government turns away from illegal duplications, then respect for the law will never lay roots in China. Rule by law is one of the most basic requirements for civilized societies.[89] Communists are famous for disregarding the need for morality. If immoral acts are encouraged on a national scale the whole nation will turn into a bunch of criminals with no hesitation to commit small and big crimes. A moral China means a police force implanted in the hearts of every one and a half billion Chinese. That is normal in the civilized world.

---

[89] I couldn't agree more to the New York Times series of editorials at the beginning of new millennium on Jan. 2000 that claimed the rule by law is one of the ten most important human achievements during the last millennium.

Anybody who sees illegal copies made by the Chinese is surprised by the sophisticated and delicate work and laments the magnificent workmanship, talent, and dedication wasted on illegal duplication. The semiconductor industry began by carving trenches on silicon plates at a width of 1/1000 millimeters. The Chinese companies presently are capable of supplying only 6% of their domestic needs for semiconductors through domestic production. They are wasting their talent with the wrong order of priority and reinforcement. It is a good example showing that a foolish ideology and a morally corrupt system can waste valuable national resources. Democracy can cure this.

## Change of Government and Economic Growth

Seventy-five years of rushing into economic growth causes fatigue even in Korea. Three times the Korean electorate voted in the progressive party to power, and gave signs of approval for their promise of higher minimum wages, automatic conversion to permanent employment from temporary jobs, nationwide free medium level education, better social welfare, and an attempt to establish a *rapprochement and engagement* with the government of North Korea even if it sacrifices nation's defense capabilities, both physically and spiritually.

But the most outstanding economic policy seeking for equity and transparency, the 'Real-Name Account System' was implemented by the conservative administration of President Kim, Young Sam. Enormous tax evasion, especially in inheritance taxes, was going on in Korea before this policy. This radical and forceful exposure of individual wealth was a deadly blow to the rich Jaebols and confused and baffled everyone because the action was taken by the conservative government. And another conservative government of President M.B. Lee designed and initiated the nationwide uniform medical insurance system in spite of the violent reaction of the Korean Medical Association, doctors and nurses alike. They invented a new phrase, *right for survival, Saeng Jon Gwon*, in Korean, but it actually meant the right for protection of monopolistic privileges. Since then, all the unions, industrial and agricultural cooperatives have used this term to fend off competition. Amazing how conservatives hate competition sometimes.

On the other hand, building a strong national security system against the Northern Communist invasion, raising the international competitiveness of Korean industries, and maintaining the healthy operation of Korea's free democratic system are three national goals that are the fundamental principles upon which this country is erected, defended, and has survived. Questioning any one of them was regarded as a cardinal sin, and denigrating them was equal to subversive treason for Koreans during most of the 20th century. The three progressive governments have invariably frightened Korean conservatives by chipping off little by little pieces of this statue of time-honored wisdom of survival in this most hostile terrain of North East Asia. But under these progressive governments, military budgets rose as in any other years and Korea became a strong arms exporter.

As Korea became more prosperous, Korean progressives found out that they are more corruptible than the so called capitalist pigs whom they hate so much, when power gave them chance for embezzlement and extortion. It seemed natural for the Korean socialists to deny not only God, but the need for moral principles to put a society together. Naturally they are divided, the immoral socialists against those who are apologetic for the low quality of their leadership.[90] At the same time the conservatives found out their three creeds are not sufficient and Korea's advanced country status has caused people to demand what the progressives claimed for Korea all along, such as minimum social welfare supports for aged population, and disabled workers and underprivileged. The conservative excuse that *'we cannot afford the improved social welfare yet'* fell apart when we found we are one of the richest of the world.

Time changes many things. But even time couldn't change two important concepts, the need for security and the drive for economic progress. In seven presidential elections, four gave power to conservatives and three to the socialists but neither side substantially departed from pursuing these two national missions. As a result we now boast one of the best (cheap and efficient) universal social medicine, a high-quality education system, a tolerable welfare system, together with world's 5th strongest military

---

[90] By nature *mediocrity* is equal to majority and excellence represent minority. If only they did not deny the value of righteousness and morality, they have excellent chance to remain in power permanently with their compassion to the losers. But they don't. Proletarian revolution seems incompatible to being Good.

power,[91] one of the most innovative technology development systems, rich and powerful economy, and the most dynamic set of corporations in the world.

In Korea, we think that there exists some sort of collective national spirit that values national development higher than other values such as equal income distribution or social safety network. Germans call it the Zeitgeist, implying literarily the Spirit of the Time. In English, the closest I can think of is the prevailing ideology, not those dichotomous minds adhering to the right or left, but the collective mind that seeks a community-wide common goal such as escaping the yoke of thousand-year-old poverty.

In Korea, progressives, as well as liberals (American Libertarians, or neo-Cons these days), put their best talents, theories, and actions into building national wealth and widespread prosperity. In spite of the oscillations of government between the pro-North Korean socialists plus the coalition of the anti-military liberals on the one hand, and

---

[91] According to the Stockholm International Peace Research Institute of Sweden Korea is 6th strongest after Japan but Korea can beat Japan easily for its Peace Constitution prohibits its owning any offensive missiles and Korean Hyun Moo series ballistic and guided missiles can reach the entire territory of Japan with EMP bombs that will send Japan back to medieval ages.

the coalition of the Korean industrialists, middle class, development generations on the other, the charts of real economic growth rates monotonically marched to the North-East. Even the most militant labor unions never denied the value of continuous growth. The pains from the war three-quarters of a century ago on this land remained so vivid and powerful that national security never lost its importance in the mind of the entire community. Koreans never suspected that their ability to produce, not to import, sophisticated high-tech weapons and this ability in turn can be acquired by improving domestic science and technology research system, and continuing the growth of the great major Korean corporations.

Korean socialist parties had several chances to nationalize major Korean industries, when they ruled the country, but they did not have the courage to nationalize great Korean corporations. During the 1997 crisis government inevitably took over the majority shares of a few major trading banks most of which they sold over to the market. More than half of the POSCO ordinary shares are in the hand of foreign investment institutions which could have been an easy target for the government takeover through superannuation fund under government control, if it wanted. We are lucky to have had mild socialists in power, who exempted us from the debilitating and expensive oscillation of nationalization and privatization.

## Role of Morality in Development

One of the uncelebrated aspects of democracy is the moral impact of this system. Speaking of the moral attributes of a political system and the role of morality in explaining economic development seems definitely out of place and the words sound like a cliché among clichés. But let me invite the readers to ask why they prefer democracy over dictatorship. The general answer will be that the former protects human rights and freedom by preventing governmental intervention in the private lives of the citizens. Then ask again why they dislike dictatorship. Authoritarian government kills innocent citizens for they overtly disagree with the policies of the government. We hate authoritarian ruling because they are immoral.

The Japanese government does not interfere with private lives and citizens remain indifferent to domestic politics. People have little reason to hate government. But Japanese people dislike the Jiminto single-party dictatorship because the Jiminto politicians do things that people hate, for example, a former prime minister sold expensive real estate owned by the government very cheap to his friend. They hate Jimminto for their immorality but vote for Jiminto because the opposition is too radical, not because they like Jiminto. Morality matters but because immoral politicians pretend that they are moral, the word became a boring cliché.

Dictatorship thrives when it is not checked, and unchecked power invariably corrupts, even in Japan, not on the same scale as the members of the CCP elites, but still substantial. *We hate dictatorship for its immorality*, and under dictatorship, there is little that people can do to stop their immoral thievery. It is fashionable among educated intellectuals to a keep distance from such an old-fashioned concept as morality in advanced rich countries. But in countries that need national development in polity, economy, and security one cannot afford to disregard morality for democracy works only when an internal checking mechanism minimizes the spreading of immorality. Democracy helps to keep society cleaner, and it ensures that the healthy middle class will continue supporting efforts to develop. When corruption is pervasive like in the defense industry of Russia and China, the country cannot protect itself from a foreign power. When the disguised dictatorship of Jiminto goes corrupt and Japanese people look the other way, even the world's second most powerful economy like Japan shrinks and sinks. Morality helps countries become and remain wealthy and powerful.

The Korean model of national development cannot be duplicated, and one doesn't need to. It was created as part of a sad and hard history. Most countries are in a much better position. Russian invasion woke up the hidden potential of the Ukraine people and the energy from the coming victory will unite the people so that they will be able to achieve great economic success. They don't have to win the war. Mere survival will give them enough motivation for prosperity and strength. When the war is over, free democracy will provoke the creativeness and resourcefulness of the citizens. They have to build a society where the intellectual resourcefulness is rewarded amply. Only one thing may come in between their present and their great prosperous future; the possibility of the corruption of the leaders and bureaucrats.

Free democracy and an unfettered free press with courageous reporters and editors will keep human greed and weakness under control. Thousands of hungry reporters in search of first-page jackpot stories of the shameful acts of powerful officials, leaders, and celebrities can minimize corruption. Communists arrest reporters in order to avoid the exposure of their crimes; the Jiminto government sends Yakusa to destroy the printing machines, criticizing the press for causing damage to their national reputation. Revelation is the cause of shame, not the crime. But countries that managed to allow freedom of the press have never failed to achieve massive prosperity.

If people seek higher incomes and wealth, if corporations seek higher technologies and growth, and if the governments are committed to raising the national level of technology and education to the highest global standards, then a country will not fail to maintain continuous economic growth. A country may not achieve these goals, but setting such goals is absolutely necessary. Pursuing an independent national defense assures peace, but there is a bonus of the new weapons industry because it helps with the acquisition of advanced technology and the development of high-tech industry. That is the unknown peace dividend that most economists miss. The peace dividend of Europe comes from reducing the defense budget, a market shrinking policy, and our peace dividend comes from increasing the defense budget, new exports, and technology advancement that is market augmenting.

It is imperative that the focus should be on making people more valuable. Only rising investments by private corporations can accomplish this. Expensive citizens in Scandinavia, with higher income and property, are proud people and their moral standards are visibly higher than the standards of Latin Americans if we believe various reports of crime rates. Korea has found that the morality and prosperity of nations are positively correlated.[92] If the comparison between the Latinos and Scandinavians is cross-section

---

[92] According to the reports of National Police Department, the Overall statistics of the Korean crime rate is generally stable over time except a visible upward shift in late 1990s due to stringent changes of the criminal law. But the rate of serious felony dropped to 1/9 during last 30 years while crime of violence such as sexual crime rose in similar rate.

evidence of this correlation, the Korean inter-temporal comparison is time-series evidence.

In March this year, a CNN reporter covering Korea aired her astonishment with a video of Korean ice cream shops, which it says are found in almost every small shopping lane in Korean cities. It is about the uniquely Korean *Unmanned Candy Shops*, where children and adults just enter, collect items they want, scan the bar codes or QR codes of the products, and drag a credit card through the card machine, then go home. I am a regular customer of such a shop and there are many unmanned shops for coffee, sandwiches, instant food, fruits, and other conveniences in Korea. I can only remember one news report about teenage vandals grabbing merchandise and having a small party without paying inside the air-conditioned shop on a hot summer night.

This is the culture of a country where their grandfathers would have raided and rampaged the shops and would have taken even the nice glass doors and refrigerators just 70 years ago. Surprisingly even foreign guest workers follow this *honor-rule shopping system*. Of course, there are CCT-

Vs installed but a base-ball cap and corona mask will make the camera useless. The number of honor-rule shops is increasing and this system is diversifying into other shops and products, probably because of the rising wage rates and corona danger from human contact. But I must submit that this is evidence for my claim that prosperity and morality are positively correlated and the causal direction goes both ways. Besides, morality is contagious too.

## Porcupine Theory of National Defense

One of the main American goals in North East Asia is neutralizing the unpredictable and ignorant North Korean regime in order to uproot the danger of its comical nuclear threat. But the neutralization of Pyeongyang will reduce the defense capability of the Northern Army of CCP by half and China can become far more vulnerable. Violent changes in North Korea will invite the direct involvement of China's land forces. That will be too messy in eliminating this second-rate power of North Korea. After the Ukrainian humiliation, Russia may become agreeable to the US plans to neutralize North Korea without messy Chinese involvement.[93]

From the vantage point of South Korea, the security situation around us has not improved much compared to 75 years ago when we started this journey of development. If anything, the danger we are in is more intense than before. As we grow bigger and stronger, we can step on the toes of any one of our neighbors, who are ready to become enemies. Our strong ally, the USA has its national interest spread all over the world and its thinly spread military power is becoming insufficient to protect Korea as China's fire power rises. Our self-defense strategy has relied too much on traditional fire power and equipment, and it has relied too much on US–made weapons imported at a very high price along with huge maintenance costs. The new security situation demanded new weapons, a new organization of the military, a new strategy, and even new friends in

---

[93] Retired four-star general of the US Army, Vincent Brooks published an article in the Foreign Affairs magazine in which he proposed this solution and expressed his hope for North Korea to know that in the long run China is its real threat, not South Korea, or the USA. Sending Vincent Brooks to Moscow and Pyeongyang as a US ambassador at large could be a good move. One of the hidden truth about the Soviet military exposed in the Ukraine war is that the corrupt Russian officers and bureaucrats made Russian high-tech weapons useless trash. China for so long illegally copied the Russian weapons and failed in achieving Russian performance levels. That makes the Chinese weapons second rate trash. China is aware of this.

this new technological age of digitalization.

One careless misstep can cause widespread destruction in this region. More than half of the world's tanks, mobile artillery, fighter aircraft, and naval ships are deployed in this region. Hostility intensifies every time China makes aggressive statements to its neighbors.

Korea does not plan to invade anybody or expand its territory by force. But it spends US$ 45 billion a year on the national defense budget, which is 6th in the world and will be 5th next year. Korea runs an army corps, called the 7th Mobile Corps, which possesses more tanks and armored vehicles than all the European countries combined. It keeps over 1000 mobile artillery weapons and 800 tanks. It has a pre-fixed order to *advance toward the North* if a war starts, and disregard any other directives that conflict with this order. The strategy is to reach Pyeongyang in 10 hours, before the Chinese army.

Defeating the North Korean military is not the main goal. Korea's main *military goal* is continuous *economic growth* and the achievement of massive prosperity. It may sound strange that the military goal is economic. This is the most important thesis that this book tries to make. *Without peace and freedom there is no prosperity, without freedom and prosperity there is no peace, and without peace and prosperity, there is no freedom or democracy.* And I submit Korea as the evidence for this claim. I would like to go on discussing this issue with examples but that will require a new book. *Suffice to say that peace, democracy and prosperity are mutually interdependent and indispensable.*

The point is that before planning for further economic growth, Korea needs a strong and viable deterrence against any attempt to start a war against us. This requires the prevention of any war on this Peninsula. Deterrence of war is the main objective of our military strategy. As we become more prosperous, we become more of a threat to surrounding powers who are used to the comfortably subservient Korea. Temptation is mounting to step on us and scotch Korea before it becomes stronger and causes headaches.

Some call it the *Porcupine Strategy, Beast Mode Strategy, or Suicidal Deterrence.* We know we cannot win a war against China, or Russia alone. This is especially so because we will not be the country that takes the first strike. All we can do is to prepare with *Deadly Retaliation Capa-*

*bility;* a retaliation effective enough to wipe out the enemy's economy, not a city or two but the entire economy. That is not an easy goal but Korea is building its fire power gradually by building weapons technology and a huge inventory of fire power. That includes the latest announcement of the Chun Moo-5 missile that carries over 15kilo ton explosives about the same to the nuclear bomb of Hiroshima without radiation.

It is reported that Korea now has an inventory of 8000 missiles and 3.5 million artillery shells inherited from the Korean War days.[94] The K9 artillery sends shells near 100 km and destroyed invading ship on the Mediterranean Sea held at a test in Egyptian shore. Nine European and Mid-Eastern countries imported this weapon from Korea. UAE is reported to have imported a range of ground-to-air intercepting missiles worth 2 and a half billion US dollars from Korea to build a new version of iron dome. Korea developed and deployed various air-to-land, land-to-air, land-to-land missiles, and ship-to-air missiles including sub-

---

[94] Korea has even invented an auto-targeting mobile canon system mounted on a truck that can start shooting in one minute. The 3.5 million howitzer shells that were almost wasted are resurrected this way. The shells are under repair adding chemical additives to raise the power of the explosion, and they are given sensors at the tips to communicate with a GPS satellite to improve their ability to hit a target.

marine-to-land missiles. The ICBM developed by Korea can fly 10,000km, and can fly in speed over 10 Mach. The semi-stealth jet fighter, K 21 is being converted into full-stealth 5th generation jet fighter. Its superior AESA radar system detects and shoots down enemy craft at 200km distance before it detects our fighter. Korean arsenal ship that carries 80missiles assisted and protected by frigates and is hidden from enemy detection can destroy several enemy cities in a single engagement. Our SLBM will effectively deliver massive retaliatory attacks to anybody who started first strike against us. Incoming missiles at the high level trajectory is intercepted by the US Thaad missiles and middle and low level skies of Korea are protected by the Korean Chun Goong missiles.

No, they are not for actual use, but for credible intimidation for effective retaliation against our potential enemies. Some air-to–ground *Korean missiles have 1000 grenade-size baby bombs inside and when all* of them explode together, an area of 200 football fields will turn to ashes. They are already deployed. *Leave us alone*, is the message. We do not want to fight with you but if you must start a war against us then be ready for massive retaliation from the ground, air, and sea, and especially from our nuclear sub-marines with SLBM for which there is no way for you to strike first. With this final addition to our arsenal, we have more or less completed our beast-mode deterrence system. Now for the first time in our history, we can assure our children that war on this Peninsula is effectively prevented. We can now talk about the future in some meaningful way, for *we will have a future here*. It should be more than a co-incidence that our grandchildren have started to hop, dance, and sing entertaining people all around the world with the Korean Wave or K-Pop. They now can enjoy themselves in ways that their aunts and uncles couldn't.

In my amateur social psychology analysis, so long as the tiger paws of the North Korea and Communist China continue threatening our back neck in close distance with mass-destruction weapons, Koreans will never slow down. Armistice, not peace, is working as the power generator of the energy for development here. Koreans, since our inde-pendence, have never experienced true peace. It is highly likely that when a real peace is accomplished on this penin-sula we may collapse. The existential danger hanging on top of our heads forces us to bury many important differences between competitors and to coexist with each other not to disturb our boat that barely keeps floating.

According to a book written by a Japanese professor, Inumiya Yoshiyuki, the 'Lead Actor's Country Korea, Supporting Actor's Country Japan' offers an amazing psychological difference between the people of Korea and Japan. The author lived in Korea and Japan alternatively for 20 years and conducted many surveys with his fellow researchers. To the following questions, the differences in responses are exceptionally revealing.

### Rate of People said Yes (%)

|  | Tokyo | Seoul |
|---|---|---|
| 1. I take the present more seriously than the future. | 28.3 | 49.4 |
| 2. I invest more to satisfy myself. | 30.3 | 43.4 |
| 3. I buy new trendy clothes. | 14.8 | 29.3 |
| 4. I buy specialty items to emphasize my individuality. | 18.9 | 31.9 |
| 5. I regularly visit well-known restaurants. | 13.1 | 46.3 |
| 6. My country is a predominantly an individualistic country. | 18.7 | 51.5 |
| 7. We handle crises together. | 32.1 | 76.3 |

Prof. Inumiya interprets the table by calling Koreans as the subjective self (like the subjective mood in a sentence) and the Japanese as the objective self. To Koreans "I" is the one and only responsible party that can determine one's future. And to the Japanese somebody else will determine the future and I am merely an object that is influenced by the party that makes the decision for me. That is one way to interpret the survey result. But I interpret them differently. This pattern of behavior is typical of people who live with daily danger consciousness and have very little expectation for the future. As the answer to question 7 clearly says, it has nothing to do with nihilism. Koreans are determined to fight against any danger or crisis but they are sadly aware of the possibility that tomorrow may not come. This is a typical warrior psychology that has been passed on from their grandparents, and it has intensified because of the quirky behavior of the North Korean regime. Finally, with our massively assured retaliation strategy or the porcupine strategy, I like to tell our grandchildren that tomorrow will come in this land most definitely.

That does not mean that the danger that threatens the existence of Korea is now fully dissipated. On the contrary, to North Korea and China, the importance of breaking South Korea has risen much higher than before. To communists, it is not possible for a militarily stronger party not to invade a weaker country, and destroy any hostile neighbor. The solution is simple. All they have to do is to dump the hostility and extend a hand of friendship and coexistence. But that is not a part of the communist agenda.

With the tips of Chinese and North Korean spears at the back of Korea's neck, all we can is to run faster and develop a superior system of defense using the ultra-high-tech science that they don't possess. That will make Korea one of the major exporters of high-tech weapons that include such new items as materials for the stealth painting for tanks and battleships, or a rail gun system that sends artillery shells at 10 Mach speeds, lithium battery-powered submarines that stay underwater for more than a month without snorkeling, or unmanned submarines that stay underwater almost forever with compressed modular nuclear reactors. We will keep the peace and prosperity that will defend our democracy.

Achieving prosperity under democracy, and a market

economy all in peace comes with an added bonus of nation-wide self-confidence and creative energy. The magnitude of what we achieved is several times greater than the arithmetic sum of what we invested in time, labor, resources, and capital. The magnitude of this unaccountable achievement beyond the higher income stream of the GDP and national net asset values of the people and institutions will be apparent in terms of Korea's ability to continue to expand the economy through technological leadership and the social desire to participate in the creation of wealth. At this moment Korea seems to be endowed with a huge amount of social energy and national collective intellect supported by a boiling communitarian desire for more achievements. Our unique model of the simultaneous achievement of the trinity of goals proved effective and will continue to be effective and no total productivity model of economic theory can explain our economic-political model of development. We have just begun.

# Appendix

## Is there an Advanced Country Stagnation Syndrome?

On July 3, 2021, the United Nations Commission of Trade and Development (UNCTAD) in Geneva officially reclassified Korea as a member of the 32-country B Group, the advanced high-income country group, and deleted it from the A Group, the middle-income countries of Asia. Two months ago, OECD in Paris announced that the Korean economy has surpassed that of Italy in per capita GDP, and has become the 8th largest economy in the world. Until last year, Korea ranked as the 11th largest economy but the corona pandemic shrank the economies of Canada, Italy, and India while the Korean economy virtually stayed the same, so the rankings changed.

On June 13, 2021, heads of the G7 Group met in Cornwall UK where the president of Korea was invited to sit in the most prominent seat, which apparently matters a lot to them. Both President Joe Biden of the USA and Prime Minister Boris Johnson of the UK wanted to replace the G7 with the D10 or D11, where D stands for the free democratic countries, including Korea, India, and Australia. It didn't happen this time due to the vehement opposition of Japan for the reason, it is reported, that Japan wants to remain the one and only Asian country in the global leadership group. Uncontrolled greed turned a positive-sum situation into a zero-sum situation. At any rate, Korea has arrived.

It has long been common sense that all advanced economies grow very slowly. In planning the future of Korea knowing what will happen to its cohorts should be the beginning. The following table is based on an OECD report on the growth performance of G7 countries.

### Real Growth Rates of G7 Economies (%)

|         | 2018 | 2019 | 2020  |
|---------|------|------|-------|
| Canada  | 1.9  | 1.5  | -8.0  |
| Germany | 1.5  | 0.5  | -6.6  |
| France  | 1.7  | 1.3  | -11.4 |
| Italy   | 0.7  | 0,0  | -11.3 |
| Japan   | 1.4  | 1.1  | -11.5 |
| UK      | 0.8  | 1.0  | -6.0  |
| USA     | 2.9  | 2.4  | -7.3  |

Source; OECD

However, OECD data also shows that G20 countries grew very aggressively, particularly, three Asian countries, India, China, and Indonesia. The Korean economy grew faster than most of the G20 countries as shown below.

## Real Growth Rates of G20 Economies (%)

|  | 2018 | 2019 |
|---|---|---|
| Argentina | -2.5 | -2.7 |
| Australia | 2.7 | 1.7 |
| Brazil | 1.1 | 0.8 |
| China | 6.6 | 6.1 |
| India | 6.8 | 5.9 |
| Indonesia | 5.2 | 5.0 |
| Mexico | 2.0 | 0.5 |
| Russia | 2.3 | 0.9 |
| Saudi | 2.2 | 1.5 |
| Turkey | 2.8 | - 0.3 |
| South Africa | 0.8 | 0.5 |

Source: OECD

## The GDP Growth rates of Korean (%)

| 2014 | 2015 | 2016 | 2017 | 2018 | 2019 | 2020 |
|---|---|---|---|---|---|---|
| 3.2 | 2.8 | 2.9 | 3.2 | 2.9 | 2.0 | -1.0 |

Should we slow down and go gently like a properly advanced country? Why don't the advanced rich countries continue to grow as Korea does? Is there an advanced country stagnation syndrome?

The world is familiar with the structural stagnation of middle-income countries. Elite-class egoism and widespread corruption in these countries are known for causing stagnation. But advanced-country stagnation seems to have different causes. In fact it is not even regarded as abnormal that rich countries grow slowly, that is until Korea arrived. As rich countries are invariably democratic, should we ask whether slow growth is a price to pay for a free democracy? Shouldn't somebody prove that democracy and freedom do not demand such an idiotic price?

It seems rich democratic countries can enjoy peace and prosperity but not growth. Their wage rate is too high to maintain a large-scale manufacturing sector. Governments are too quick to take the easy options of seeking alternative industries like tourism than trying to generate new employment through the hard option of technological progress and competitive manufacturing. You don't have to invest in building another old palace. Economists even claim that technological progress is possible without investing in the ecologically unfriendly manufacturing industry. To a certain extent, blind faith in the global value chain network demonstrates that it indeed is possible, at the expense of the environment of the poor. Under the present level of manufacturing technology, somebody's environment must be roughed up to host a competitive manufacturing sector, in order to save somebody else's environment.

But repeated easy options have proven to be extremely short-sighted. No matter how advanced the US scientists are in designing sophisticated semiconductors, if they have to rely on Korea and Taiwan for production, the US is in a very dangerous situation. There are a dozen reasons why the transportation of unfinished products across the Pacific can be disrupted. If China really wants to own TSMC and its semiconductor technologies, the only way for the US to prevent it is to go to war against China, or destroy TSMC. Either way, it is a very precarious situation. The new world of advanced product technology without the support of advanced production technology will thrive only in scholastic brains.

The table below is borrowed from an OECD report and shows that no rich and advanced democracy has a government budget lower than 46% of its GDP. The governments that spend nearly half of their GDP are all concentrated in western and central Europe except for Brazil, an anomaly for a big socialist government. Further investigation shows that all the high-spending governments allocate a high portion of their budgets for debt-servicing, social welfare, and unemployment benefits. These expenses do not promote economic growth as much as the expenditures related to industrial promotion, infrastructure, and technological and military research grants. That leaves technological development and economic growth mostly to the private sector. Governments of rich countries proved to be too poor to care for to the private sector technology development.

## Government Budget over GDP (%)

(Percentage of GDP)

| Country | Spending as % | Revenue as % | Deficit as % |
|---------|---------------|--------------|--------------|
| Canada  | 52.4          | 41.7         | -10.7        |
| Denmark | 55.1          | 51.6         | - 3.5        |
| France  | 62.4          | 52.5         | - 9.9        |
| Germany | 51.9          | 46.9         | - 4.2        |

| | | | |
|---|---|---|---|
| Italy | 57.3 | 47.8 | - 9.5 |
| Japan | 46.7 | 34.0 | -12.6 |
| Norway | 58.2 | 51.2 | - 6.9 |
| Sweden | 53.1 | 49.1 | - 4.0 |
| UK | 50.2 | 36.8 | -13.4 |
| USA | 46.2 | 30.3 | -15.8 |

Source; OECD

# Appendix

# The American Exceptionalism in Industrial Growth

The American growth rate is rare among rich countries. It has a real growth rate as high as 4.5%. I call this the American Miracle. America seems to have broken the wall; the wall of slow growth in rich countries with poor governments. The first distinction is the military spending, particularly the defense industry research programs, and the second is the introduction of new platform industries that pool the entire global population into becoming one mutually dependent member of a single community.[95]

---

[95] Healthy demographic structure of America is often quoted as the reason for the higher

American leaders complain with various shades of dissatisfaction that the NATO governments are free-riding taking advantage of American military spending. Europeans are smart to have the USA handle most of the military budget for NATO but Americans, I believe, are smarter, for they recovered their spending from their supreme military technology for which there is no match in the world. A substantial part of the 3.5% of GDP (over 700 billion dollars every single year) that goes into the Pentagon mostly flows out to the private sector high-tech companies that in turn gets outsourced to a wide range of private American manufacturing industries. Even the tidal wave and global fashion of value chains haven't cracked the military-industrial complex, for sensitive military-related technologies cannot cross the borderlines. It was not the lack of a European Steve Jobs or Elon Musk that caused European stagnation, but it was the lack of a European Pentagon with talented individuals who can scare the congressmen with the dangerous scenario if enough money is not spent. Europeans killed each other by tens of millions less than a century ago, and it is very hard to crack their aspiration for peace

---

growth, but we will skip it for it opens an entirely new world of debate that is beyond this book.

and scare them to focus on military buildup, even if it is false security.

Please, don't take me wrong. I am not suggesting the European countries should start spending a huge amount of their budget on military spending and kill each other. I am merely pointing out that Korea plans to spend little less than 50 billion US dollars this year and over 300 billion during the next five years and more than half of it will be spent on new acquisitions. The free-riding European security system may not be so smart considering all the opportunities they gave up in high technology development. The Russian invasion of Ukraine highlighted the European governments' foolishness in the false parsimony on defense. They are now joining the queue for booking South Korean weapons, and one of them, Polish Defense Department just contacted a 21 Billion dollars purchase agreement with Korean weapon makers for 1000 tanks, 600 mobile automatic howitzers, and 48 supersonic jet fighters.

Any businessman with a gram of interest in technology would understand that the defense industry demands advanced electronics, mechanics, new materials, welding of rare metals, chemistry, bioscience, computers, communications, semiconductors, display technologies, aerodynamics, radar technology, laser science, and sonar technology. The forward and backward linkage effects of the   weapons industry gives wonderful opportunities for accelerated economic growth in advanced economies.

Western governments prefer to import proven American weapons and products, whereas their government defense budget by nature gives a guarantee to the domestic acquisition if the domestic economy can produce them. Besides American weapon makers have limited capacity for production just as in any industry. Ukraine war exhausted the American excess capacities for weapon making according to the American government. While the Chinese navy and air force   surrounded Taiwan Island and staged a military exercise with real bullets and missiles, the US government refused to sell weapons for the defense of Taiwan, because it ran out of inventory to sell. And there are very limited alternative sources that supply weapons with similar performance to the American weapons.

The US manufacturing sector survived well during the

China rush. The European manufacturing sector fell into a long-term slumber, and when they awakened by the corona-pandemic travel bans, they discovered that they were unable to produce even such simple products as PCR test kits and medical-quality facial masks. New products such as vaccines developed at home can be wasted if everybody has to go to China for mass production. Ten years ago Korea was completely void of bio-science industries, but today it has the world's largest bio-similar industry. Any European countries could have done the same during the same time but they didn't.

The second distinctive road that the US corporations took is their creative efforts of taking advantage of the super-connectivity of economic players i.e. consumers, governments, and corporations. During the ten-year period after 2010, the American manufacturing sector lost over 5.03 million jobs and new industries that are related to internet connectivity absorbed roughly the same number of workers. Apple with a 2.177 trillion dollar market capitalization, Google ($1.668 trill.), Microsoft ($1.657 trill.), and Amazon ($1.607 trill.) are the four largest alternative industry employers followed by Facebook, Tencent, Alibaba, Tesla, and Netflix. They are the new generation champions. While the market capitalization values of these high-tech companies are typically about ten times greater than the traditional companies such as GE, JP Morgan, Boeing, Johnson, etc. their contributions of new employment are no more than one-tenth of the employment of these top-ranking traditional companies. An important fact is that none of these companies, not even as a concept, existed before the internet was popularized in the 1990s. To the European and Japanese major corporations or individuals, the profit opportunities of the new, quick and easy connectivity apparently looked far smaller compared to the risk and expenses associated with the entrance. Or were they simply complacent?

The remarkable distinction of these new players is not only their large market capital value that expresses the public expectation as to how big they may grow in time, but nearly all of them are so-called *platform businesses* that cannot exist without the hyper-connectivity. They are also called a common ecology-based businesses in which members invariably share the ecology, ownership of the business, and final profit with the owner of the platform, the mother company. Residents of the ecology typically range over 100 million, far greater than the medium-sized European and Latin American countries, and each member and the mother company simply do their best to make good profits using individual creativity while helping the ecology to grow in strength and size. It seems to be a good business that cannot fail.

But blue skies never last long. Apple is reported to have borrowed 50 billion dollars in 2020 to buy back its own shares from the market. In 2019 alone 46.0 billion dollars were used for the same purpose. Apple has done the same for last 10 years and the total buy-back fund borrowed is over 1.84 trillion dollars. This is 20% greater than the GDP of Korea, and there are about 200 countries whose GDPs are less than this. The trouble is that Google is also doing the same on a slightly smaller scale. The EBITAD (earnings before interest, tax, and depreciation) dropped from 35.9% in 2010 to 25.0% in 2013. Exceptionally high profit performance entailed exceptionally high market capitalization, which is nearly impossible to sustain if profit rates start to drop. As the operational profits drop continuously because competitors appear all around, a company starts to issue indirect dividends by buying up their own company stock in the market. The Fed was very helpful by providing a generous liquidity supply but the good times are over with high interest rates, high energy and grain price. But America does not worry me. The new frontiers of technology will supply more opportunities.

# XII. Opportunities for Korea

## Changes in New International Relations

The Cold War, in retrospect, was a series of challenges to American superiority by changing adversaries of the Eurasian continent. The first challenger was the Soviet Union led by Stalin and his followers from the end of WWII. This lasted until 1992 when the Soviet Union disintegrated. Since then the US-Russia relationship was cold but not a war until Putin resurrected the War in 2000 through his invasion of Ukraine. But in this battle of Russian attrition in Ukraine, Putin effectively extinguished any hope for more Russian challenges to the US. Not a single boot of US soldiers touched the ground of Ukraine and the US government spent about three percent of its annual defense budget by supplying advanced weapons to Ukraine's military. History will record this as the most *economic* victory.

The other Eurasian challenger is Maoist China. It started the hostility to the US from its inauguration in 1949 and actually fought against the US Army in the Korean War (1950 -1953). The combined Sino-Russo challenge to the US and the American humiliation in Vietnam drained US supremacy substantially, and President Nixon had to start a *detent* with Beijing in 1972. This Sino-US honeymoon pushed China's economy to the number two position in the size of GDP after America through the introduction of a market economy in China and the optimization of the global value-chain of manufactured goods. Xi, Jin Ping became arrogant at this remarkable accomplishment and restarted the Cold War against the US in 2017 declaring that China's economy will surpass the US's by 2030, and will unify Taiwan by force. With this China Dream, he earned his third 5-year term.

Technically, America is in a Cold War with both of them now, but for all practical purpose, it is over. In modern warfare where precision explosives can be delivered to every corner of the world on a stealth carrier, the ability to detect the location of enemy force, the size, and firepower before the enemy, determines the winner. It makes you a sniper with a high-tech weapon fighting against a blind man with a knife. China knows that it is this blind man. With the American semiconductor design technology, Taiwanese fabrication capability, and Korean memory and precision optic technology that China doesn't possess, China is no match in the coming battles.

The founder of the Samsung Group practically devoted his life in establishing a Korean semiconductor industry, whereas for Korea in total, it was a stroke of inadvertent luck that one of our corporate leaders had a farsighted vision from early 1980. Even American and Chinese leaders didn't understand the importance of this industry until the latter part of the 2010s. Achieving a stable supply line of system chips and memories guarantees entry into the connected society that will make use of great new technologies such as AI, 6th-generation telecommunications, supercomputers, robotics, and unmanned transport equipment. Without such a supply line, like in China, you can be a good consumer but not the supplier. Makers of chips can determine the winners against losers in the future. CCP can survey its citizens with a hundred million cameras, but it cannot survey the citizens of the world. For that, they need better technology and chips.

## Do not Predict the Future, Make it

Growth is not a goal for the Korean economy any more. It will be merely a byproduct of nationwide changes that deeply alters the way people think, work, learn and live. There is no point to resist this trend. Either you lead the changes or follow behind others.

With this backdrop, Korea discovered that it is situated on a unique coordinate in the race to the hyper-connected society. It is a great irony that a platform company that builds a huge ecology for a million participants is fatally dependent on services and devices of much smaller analogue companies. Digital data centers have to be *constructed* and supplied with *computer hardware* and electricity that is basically an analog activity. Korean companies have taken their positioning on most analogue industries to provide concurrent services for the operation of huge platform companies. One good example of this category is Coupang, the ubiquitous, unicorn Korean shopping mall with *fast de-*

*livery-system*. It started in Korea and is now jointly owned together with German and Japanese companies soon to be listed on the New York Stock Exchange. Analogue services are indispensable for digital efficiency. Like the von Neumann bottleneck of data processing, no digital service can be faster than the analogue delivery system.

Likewise without device manufacturing industries, such as unmanned vehicles, connectivity would remain just connectivity. Device is a generic term for the hardware part of a system. Computers, semiconductors, memory chips and all sorts of processing units and systems, undersea glass wiring, sensors and cameras, and 5th and 6th generation data delivery systems are parts of the hardware system that senses, recognizes, computes and make decisions, and sends back data to the functioning devices. Without the sophisticated system of integrated command control, modern stealth fighter planes are just hunks of metal, and without the actual fighter craft, the software systems are just a collection of digital statements. For the advanced digital economies, hard device manufacturing is indispensable.

Korea took this manufacturing territory as its main playground. We are several steps behind all the great research institutes and laboratories of the USA and Europe in brain researches and computer designs. While the great western institutes have the better alternatives such as AI-based research, and global scale platforms for exchanges of twits, faces, and memos, even block-chained coins, Korea had to wrestle with the boring manufacturing industry, for that's what we can do better than Google, Amazon and Facebook and that's the analogue world.

At this turning point of our economy from one based on manufacturing to one based on information and connectivity, Korea and other economies need to make major decisions that could cause a fatal difference down the road. High wage costs in rich countries, environmental limitations posed by governments, and the easy option of value-chain popularity (Let-the-Chinese-Make-It Mind Set) in many rich countries, has given a wide-open opportunity to Korea.

## Green Energy Initiatives

The EU Commission announced that after 2035 no

more combustion engine vehicles will be produced in EU member countries. It is equivalent to preventing cars from burning carbon on the European roads. This was a shock to all the carmakers, especially to Japanese carmakers. But in general most of the European, Korean, and Chinese carmakers did anticipate the end of carbon-burning-fuming vehicles and have been preparing themselves for this for some time. This is one of the most powerful responses to the visibly deteriorating climate of the earth. Governments of leading countries are determined to cut down, if not completely stop, the carbon energy consumption and this trend marks the future global economy in which Korea must compete and survive.

Unlike other mature rich countries that derive their wealth from finance, tourism, resources, and service industries, the Korean economy is based on rapidly growing manufacturing industries and suffers from massive pollution generated both in and out of Korea. Korea's priority lies in inventing new ways to manufacture the same goods with lower carbon burning and power consumption rather than cutting down the level of economic activities. Naturally, Korea leads the world in the nickel–cobalt-manganic lithium battery technology particularly in the delicate high energy-density cathode manufacturing.

LG Energy Solutions, SK Innovation, and POSCO Chemicals the three largest lithium battery makers in Korea are competing with the Chinese CATL for the leadership in the mobile source of energy for electric cars in the post-carbon era. SDI, a member of the Samsung Group just announced that it perfected the commercial use of solid lithium battery which is inflammable with commercially acceptable energy intensity. The three Korean battery makers supply to most of the American and European carmakers, and CATL supplies mainly Chinese carmakers.

Over eighty percent of Chinese power plants burn coal that used to be imported from Australia, and the post-Fukushima Japan shut down their nuclear power plants and half of their power now comes from coal-burning power plants. Unusually massive rainfall in 2020 on the large population centers of China and the Japanese Archipelago raised the suspicion that abnormal precipitation may have some correlation with the amount of carbon generated by burning coal. Korea's answer to this problem is to design SMR (Small Modular Reactor) and use it for small scale power plants in fixed-places or in mobile power plants in ships, submarines and space rockets. It reduces the harmful radiation more than the size-reduction of reactors and probability of accidents declines by a factor of 1 over a hundred million. The Korean Atomic Energy Commission built one and had it approved by the US Office of Nuclear Energy, Safety and Security to ensure its safety and reliability. That opens the door to a huge export markets and the world can become safer with more power.

Cars can call for help when the lithium battery they use catches fire, but if there is fire on ships or airplanes while in operation on the ocean or in the air, it is fatal. Therefore the substitution of diesel engines by electric motors for ships and planes cannot begin until the lithium-battery fire problem is fully resolved. The source of fire in batteries is the liquid electrolyte within the batteries and the vanadium-ion battery uses ordinary water as its electrolyte; therefore it is safe from fire. Hyundai Motor Co. and Standard Technology, both Korean companies, announced that they would jointly develop a commercial version of an electric motor for ships and airplanes using this vanadium-ion battery. The proto-type samples are under test for durability and safety.

In the coming new world data will be a factor of production like capital and labor. To the normal and ordinary minds like us, data are new resource that helps us in making people more comfortable, happy, predictable and wealthy. To the twisted minds of communists, data seems the source of power and control therefore should be handled as scarce resource. By controlling data they think they can control the society and people. Generating and utilizing data are free in free societies. When *Abatas* start speaking freely in *Metaverses*, we are bound to consume immensely more power and burn something. Cheap and clean energy technology will give the key for leadership in the coming world.

## Making Future by Fusing Industries

Korea discovered fusing information-society technology with traditional manufacturing technologies opens huge new opportunities. This is a God-given opportunity equally open to any country that is willing to make its manufacturing sector grow by fusing digital technologies easily accessible. But only some took the opportunity and moved quicker than the rest.

The concept of *fusing industries* is an outcome of constant worry about the future leading industries on a global scale. The prime example is the iPhone of Apple. Automobiles used to be the most fused industry involving technologies and parts from numerous industries. It even created a community of billion drivers many of whom became loyal members of the same brand. But they only drove, whereas the loyal members of the iPhone community constantly make the future together with Apple by creating new apps and spreading them by forcing or enticing receivers of communication to install the new functions. It is like the royal car drivers joining in creating new flying cars.

Korea's portfolio in the manufacturing sector was modest in early 2000 with very basic industries like cars, trucks, parts, shipbuilding, industrial machinery, railroads and railcars, household electronics, analog style tanks and artillery, pilot training jet fighters, and petrochemical and petroleum plants. The major global market share for all of these industries was occupied by global giants several times bigger than Korean players. Participation on a massive scale by Chinese manufacturers turned the red oceans even redder. No room existed for Korean manufacturers to grow any further unless Korea starts making the same things differently or making new things by fusing digital technology. Fusing industries suddenly became part of the fixed menu in the economic manifesto of Korean political candidates.[96]

National anxiety about the next generation leadership industry and the way people regard Korea's major corporations as some sort of national champions like athletes provided a unique national sense of common destiny, Korean Communitarianism. The oligopolistic Jaebols have become effective catalytic agents for chemical fusions of various industries. Manufacturing plants owned by Korean companies in China and Vietnam are returning back to Korea. Their new plants in Korea are inevitably equipped with automatic high-tech machines and systems to compete against the products of cheap-wage countries.

The AI-driven integrated bus service management sys-

---

[96] One dean of the Seoul National University, Graduate school of Fusion Science ran for the Presidential election three times. He earned close to one hundred million dollars from his startup of fusing technology.

tem of major cities of Korea is an excellent example of digital technology fused with the transportation industry. This is one extraordinary example involving the fusion of a ground transportation system which is an analog industry, with an AI data management system which is digital. The life of a metropolitan bus-route company boss is tough and full of struggles with his bus drivers. He has never heard a word like digitalization in his life. Whether he knows or not, above the sky of Seoul there hangs a huge invisible cloud of digital information that (1) the central and local computers receive, process, and redistribute, in real-time, new set of data generated by the cards tagged on the LCD displays by millions of bus-riding clients, (2) that each tagging reveals the stations where clients got on and off the bus with which the computer calculates the fair for each client and deduct from either the traffic card balance that was tagged or from the client's bank account if the client used his or her cash card, while (3) the displays installed on the bus and every bus station shows the location of each bus and how long it would take for all the buses approaching to come to all the stations, and a sweet voice of a lady announces the information of time needed for arrival or arrival warning.

The fare collection system is equally digital. A small 10 cm x 10 cm digital POS box is waiting to scan your cash card, T-money card, or credit card to deduct the fare from your bank account. The system automatically computes the discounts made available by law or regulation for students and elders. It even computes the transfer discounts to passengers going in the same direction after transferring from subways and buses. Amazingly this system discretely prevents the exposure of the total balance of my bank account by showing only a part of it, so long as it is sufficient to cover my fare, but in the case of traffic card, it shows the exact amount of the remaining balance to help the client.

Foreign visitors are regularly impressed by the precision of the displayed arrival information of buses that they are waiting to catch at each bus station, but they should wonder more about the speed at which the information displayed is collected, computed, and redistributed. Literarily tens of thousands of buses constantly move around in the metropolitan Seoul sending continuous flow of precise information regarding the movements of buses and passengers. Different new information about the bus locations, and their movements are sent to thousands of station displays with new set of information in less than five seconds. The amount of information traffic and the speed of massive computation with precision is mind-boggling. But compared to what the digital technology can provide in the future this is merely a beginning.

This is an example of fusing the digital system-engineering industry, subway industry, bus industry, display device industry, computer and cloud service industry of IDCs (Internet Data Centers), and the credit card and banking industry. It is hard to imagine where this hyper-connectivity may lead us in the future. One thing is certain. It will come in forms that fuse industries, products, and services. The same hardware like buses and subway cars are doing whatever they were made to do, but the way the same hardware serves you becomes different by fusing new digital functions and services, which in turn create demand for new devices and hardware. Industrial fusion has arrived silently, but the impact is loudly visible, and it is making your life substantially more convenient, although the mechanism is hiding behind the invisible cloud.

It will be unfair to finish this chapter without mentioning the extraordinary role played by the Korean entertainment industry in the construction of modern Korea. I will not try to explain the causes of the popularity of K-pop, K-drama, K-cinema, K-food, and K-culture. To my biased eyes this K popularity is but one more example of the timely fusion of many formerly unrelated industries such as semiconductors, computers, and communication through internet connectivity with popular music that used to be delivered to the consumers through CDs, long-play disks, and concerts that required physical attendance. It has taken more than twenty years since the World Wide Web (www.) started to connect the entire world before Korean pop music videos suddenly became popular all over the world.

During this long period of time anybody, particularly the Hollywood movie industry, could have conquered the world through an internet delivery system but they did not. Instead the K-pop wave, which was followed by K-drama and other K-entertainment forms did that. The business part of K-drama is virtually monopolized by Netflix, an American internet entertainment company. Therefore the K-culture phenomenon is a result of the successful fusion of American business skills and technology of internet delivery, with the

Korean capability of making entertaining content for the world. The Korean ability in making entertaining content comes from the creative fusion of the techniques of story-telling, visual presentation, computer graphics, very talented acting and directing.

Fusion is a poor-man's solution to the rapid technology change in the digital and metaverse world. We chose to supply the necessary logistic support from the analog world, where our eyes, ears, and mouth live. The digital revolution is at the beginning stage, and there exists a great space for all the developing countries. Hesitation in digital initiation can exclude a country eternally from the rapid train of changes because digitalization means doing things in new ways. But by neglecting the manufacturing sector one can become a captive of other manufacturing country.

# Appendix

## A Theory of Trinity in National Development

At the end of this book, readers will find, I hope, that

Korea to is an extraordinary example of a new theory, the *Trinity in National Development* in action. It is based on the commonly known examples of *failed economic growth*. India, Pakistan, Nigeria, Sierra Leon, and Afghanistan testify that where there is no peace, mass prosperity cannot be achieved. Where there is no general freedom for the citizens and no free press and transparency in society, mass prosperity has never been achieved like in the Soviet Union and North Korea. If part of the society achieved limited prosperity like the party officers of communist China, it cannot last for the society quickly turns into a corrupt plutocracy characterized by a *nationwide competitive corruption*. Poor countries all over the world fail to keep their democracy and peace for they lack the resources to defend their country and domestic politics continue unstable.

It is apparent that a strong ability to effectively deter any war on one's territory, namely the ability to keep the *peace* is essential for sustained economic growth. It is equally apparent that without the *democratic political system* that guarantees individual property ownership, and freedom of speech to maintain social transparency and control the corruption of political leaders at a reasonable level, a society cannot achieve lasting economic development. There are many examples that fall into this category among Central Asian countries. Furthermore, there is simply no example where massive nationwide prosperity is achieved in a society in which there is no *free market economy*. The Korean experience shows that the three blessings come in one package like the Holy Trinity. During the war in the early 1950s, we didn't realize that *the campaign to drive out the Communist invaders was our first step to lay the groundwork for subsequent national development and mass prosperity.*

In today's world, peace, namely living among friendly nations, is a luxury, and in all practical terms preventing a war on one's territory is an outstanding achievement in itself because countries are so easily tempted to enter into all sorts of conflicts against each other for surprisingly unimportant causes. If you are militarily weak, your strong neighbors are likely to use your territory as their battleground. All of Europe experienced that during WWII. To build such military strength to fend off the quarrelling parties, you need a strong economy and industrial power. Without lasting peace, the economy cannot grow, and Korea has benefited from the cease-fire status for the past 70 years. That was a blessing for Koreans. Without sufficient power to deter an invasion, economic development is impossible, and without building strong economic power an effective deterrence against war cannot be built either.

Without any sophisticated explanations, Koreans knew instinctively by looking at the Soviet Union and North Korea that the free market system, that private property, and transparency are the critical and indispensable conditions for achieving economic growth and mass prosperity. A free market system, private property, and transparency under a democratic political system minimize the widespread corruptions of powerful individuals in power, military, media, and industry. Without this societal cleansing mechanism properly functioning, these greedy elements constantly try to institutionalize their special privileges to protect their secret sources of illegal earnings. By colluding with each other, they quickly turn the society into a rigid authoritarian system. In the beginning, it was the economic gains that tempted them to help each other under the table but soon they find that monopolizing power is a far easier way to perpetuate their illegal gains. The state falls into the hands of organized crimes and economic growth stops.

Let's deal with the sufficient condition. In Latin American countries, there is neither a war going on nor a lasting dictatorship. But even with the free market system, economic growth is not sustained. Poor economic achievement constantly threatens democracy and social stability. Venezuela is a good example. They enjoy peace, freedom, and a market economy, but not sustained economic growth. Is this an exception to the rule of the Trinity? The fact is that the trinity is a set of necessary conditions.

The sufficient condition is in establishing a stable and sufficiently large middle class with individuals who are reasonably rich, share the national aspiration for mass prosperity, and support a healthy democratic system that is sensitive to the demands of the underprivileged class. If peace, a market economy, and freedom are guaranteed, and if the nation succeeds in building a healthy middle class that supports a democratic system, and if the entire nation is dedicated to the goal of mass prosperity as well, it will be very hard to fail in sustained economic growth and prosperity. Most of the European countries and Korea fall into this category. But a healthy middle class with reasonable wealth cannot exist before mass prosperity is achieved. Therefore it cannot be a necessary condition.

Japan is an interesting case. It is endowed with peace, free democracy, and prosperity under a market economy with a system of private property ownership. It even has a large and stable middle class. But it is trapped in long-term stagnation. One element that Japan does not possess is freedom of expression. Japan inherited a very special culture from the Samurai days; an enormous social power of conformity. The whole society quietly demands general suppression of dissension in the name of national interest and harmony. Dissident journalism is punished ruthlessly by politically biased organized criminals. Japan does not have freedom of speech. If a boss is discovered while stealing, his secretary, who knows all the details of the crime, commits suicide to protect his immoral boss. The company is protected from media exposure, and other members of the company respect the secretary. Any creativeness is suppressed and *gradual improvement or Kaisen* without rocking the boat has become the rule. The democratic political system of Japan cleverly eliminated the civic rights and responsibilities to supervise and criticize rulers. It is a democracy only in forms and seriously fails to satisfy one of our necessary conditions.

China is easy to explain using this theory. It enjoys peace of a kind but seriously lacks in freedom of nearly everything except the right to make money. Private property ownership is tolerated by the party but only so far. Mild public criticism of the party policy by one of the richest businessmen entailed his loss of a majority share of his company in a form of voluntary donation.[97] Dissention against the party policy by an ordinary citizen invites death. The media is simply a device for public relations for the party and a tool for general indoctrination. In normal countries, the government is a tool for the people to achieve the national goals but in China, people are tools for achieving party goals. Obedience, not creativity, is what the party demands from people. Even a small disturbance in the supply of coal or semiconductors easily paralyzes the whole country. The market economy usually prepares for anticipated shortages but not in China.

---

[97] Ma Win is the most successful Chinese businessman who built the Alibaba Empire by importing the digital shopping mall platform before most of the world, let alone Chinese. He seemed to have forgotten that he is Chinese when he mildly criticized the authoritarian policy of the China Central Bank. He disappeared from the public for a couple of months and he announced the donation of his company share to the Communist Party of China.

There is simply no example of achieving mass prosperity under an authoritarian dictatorship in modern human history. There is no example of achieving prosperity for a country in a war. *We need peace for opulence.* Inversely there is no example where a weak and poor country developed an independent military defense system. *We need opulence for peace.* Small and prosperous but weak countries without an independent military defense system have to rely on some sort of expensive diplomatic arrangement for their safety. Poverty does not guarantee peace, for poor countries cannot defend themselves independently. Unfortunately strong rogue states are never in short supply and joint security treaties never proved fully reliable for powerful and friendly neighbors such as the USA either suffer from budget shortages or hesitate to come to rescue a small partner under threat of invasion, lest the regional conflict develops into a major war or WWIII. Ukraine shows the needs as well as the limitation of joint security treaties.

*We need democracy for peace.* Autocrats usually lead the country into war whenever they find themselves unpopular among their own people. *We need peace for democracy* for a country in war tends to concentrate power in the hands of autocrats. *We need democracy for sustained economic growth,* for under a strong government economy grows only when the country is very poor but as soon as the economy goes into the middle-income stage, without the active corporate brains who have better exposure to international competition, the country cannot survive the severe export competition. All the communist countries of the world proved that. *We need active economic growth for democracy to settle down,* for slow growth entails militant labor union activism and alienation of the middle class. The nation turns into a battleground of class confrontation to get more of the fixed pie. This book explained that the statements are true through the Korean experience.

There were times in Korea when only two or one of the conditions were met. Korean success was possible only because Koreans were forced to achieve the three objectives simultaneously. We had to defend our country and had to maintain our democracy, and millions were killed for it. Strong military deterrence is a consequence of high economic growth but it is also the cause of rapid industrialization by ensuring a peaceful circumstance. Although we did not know then, it has become obvious that we haven't had any other option but to become wealthy and strong just to survive. That is a paradoxical anomaly. We didn't have the privilege to be strong and democratic but poor or to be democratic and rich but weak.

# Epilogue

That brings us to the enlightening lecture of professor Odd A. Westad of Harvard University titled *Empire and Righteous Nation 600 Years of China-Korea Relations*, The Edwin O. Reischauer Lectures. He does not say that Korea is righteous and China is not. He raises the question of how Korea survived the long history of independence while living as a neighbor of an over-whelming China. He says nationalism and clever diplomacy of Korea helped. But at the center of the relationship, there always existed Yi, or Ye in Korean, the Neo-Confucian respect to the harmony and orderliness of society by following the rule of loyalty, respect, trust, and love. Few will disagree with him. Throughout the history of the bilateral relationships, there was unending mutual respect.

Whether the professor was aware or not, in the west, when one uses the word righteousness, it connotes a moral principle. It should be used with a clear reason why an act is good or bad. In Christendom, the source of righteousness comes from the absolute virtue of God. In communism, which denies the existence of God, this criterion for absolute value disappears. Righteousness is what party says. In Confucian morality, virtue comes from the rule of human relations called Ye. This moral relativism also applies to the Shinto religion of Japan. Such a lack of respect for absolute virtue makes people believe that acceptance by the community one belongs is of the highest value. Sino-centrism can be the ultimate rule overpowering other values such as mercy, friendship, or even love.

In a community where people believe in the existence of absolute virtue, whether it is through Christianity or Buddhism, material well-being seems to raise the moral consciousness of the residents. In a community where intellectual elites devote more time to researching why a free society based on individual liberty must decay, and take pride in becoming the advanced guard of a *decadent* culture, moral standards and prosperity have to be inversely correlated. Don't blame immigrants and colored class. Intellectual elites promote hatred and subversion of the universally accepted human values in these countries in the name of freedom.

People in a morally conscious society take pride in being financially independent. Millions of self-employed papas and mamas of Korea deserve special mention for their indomitable spirit of independence. Korean unemployment benefits and superannuation benefits are so inadequate that after retirement at around late fifty or early sixty most Koreans have to start some form of business that barely generates money for *wages* the owners could have earned elsewhere. The percentage of the self-employed occupies 24.6% of the total employment in Korea, and that is the highest among the industrial countries.[98] The sight of their disorderly and ugly sign boards competing for your attention on many buildings of Korean cities testifies to the intensity of their competition for survival. One-quarter of the total employment is generated by self-employment and that works as an important social cushion, and the shop owners are rewarded with the pride of remaining in the independent middle class even if it may last for only a couple of

---

[98] The same number for USA is 6.3%, 8.6 for Canada, 9.6 for Germany, 10.0 for Japan, 12.4 for France according to OECD.

years.

Pearl S. Buck is a literary Nobel laureate who had a special love for China and Korea. On one autumn evening twilight she was walking on a Korean country road when she met an old tired farmer who was tugging on a rope tied to an old ox that pulled a wagon with some bundles of rice straw. What attracted its interest was that the farmer also carried on his back an A-frame loaded with a bundle of rice straw. She asked, through an interpreter, why he wasn't riding the wagon and putting his load on the wagon. The answer was "I shouldn't do that. My ox worked the whole day for me and is more tired than me."

If you find the old man irrational, I respect you, for you are a rational reader who knows how to maximize human happiness. But if you find the old man's behavior agreeable, I respect you even more, for you know how to share your happiness. Sharing happiness is the key that will help you understand the Korean peculiarities, social energy and its communitarianism. If pretending that there is communal harmony by suppressing individual emotion and individualities is the measure of maturity, Koreans will never be mature. The empathy to the weaker members of the community or even strangers is the character of independent people living in a mature society and Korean people have great difficulty in leaving anybody behind. And they call it the Jeong.

Repeating the Korean Economic Miracle
# NEW WEALTH OF NATIONS

First Edition : Sep.   4th, 2023
     Printed : Sep. 12th, 2023

Copyright 2023 by Ungsuh Kenneth Park
Publisher : Seo Young Ae,
          Daeyang Media

#602 Ilho Bldg., 22-6 Toegye-ro 45-gil, Jung-gu, Seoul Korea (04559)
Tel : 822-2276-0078
Fax : 822-2267-7888

ISBN 979-11-6072-115-7 03320

20,000KRW